Christian

The
Confident
Christian

Seeing with the eyes of faith

DR. GARY L. HARBAUGH

NORTHERN LIGHTS INTERNATIONAL
MINISTRY

4 2 5 - 7 4 2 - 2 5 3 5

4 2 5 - 3 3 7 - 3 6 9 8

Augsburg

MINNEAPOLIS

THE CONFIDENT CHRISTIAN
Seeing with the eyes of faith

Copyright © 2000 Gary L. Harbaugh. All rights reserved. Except for brief quotations in critical articles or reviews, no part of this book may be reproduced in any
manner without prior written permission from the publisher. Write to: Permissions,
Augsburg Fortress, Box 1209, Minneapolis, MN 55440.

Adapted from *The Faith-Hardy Christian: How to Face the Challenges of Life with
Confidence,* copyright © 1986 Augsburg Publishing House.

A Biblical Model of Wholeness is copyright © 1983 Gary L. Harbaugh, Ph.D.
Faith-Hardiness Inventory is copyright © 1984 Gary L. Harbaugh, Ph.D.

Myers-Briggs Type Indicator, MBTI, is a registered trademark ® of Consulting Psychologists Press, Palo Alto, California, 94303.

The Holmes-Rahe Social Readjustment Scale is copyright © 1997 Richard
Rahe, M.D., and used by permission.

Unless otherwise indicated, scripture quotations are taken from the Holy Bible, New
International Version (NIV) copyright © 1973, 1978, 1984 International Bible Soci-
ety. Used by permission of Zondervan Publishing House. All rights reserved. The
"NIV" and "New International Version" trademarks are registered in the United
States Patent and Trademark Office by International Bible Society. Use of either
trademark requires the permission of International Bible Society.

Scripture quotations marked TEV are from the Good News Bible, Today's English Version, copyright © 1966, 1971, 1976 by American Bible Society. Used by permission.

Scripture from The New English Bible is copyright © 1961, 1970 by the Delegates
of the Oxford University Press and the Syndics of the Cambridge University Press.
Reprinted by permission.

Scripture quotations marked KJV are from The New King James Version, copyright
© 1979, 1980, 1982 Thomas Nelson, Inc. Used by permission. All rights reserved.

Cover photograph copyright © 2000 Tony Stone Images. Used by permission.
Cover design by Derek Herzog
Book design by Timothy W. Larson

Library of Congress Cataloging-in-Publication Data

Harbaugh, Gary L.
  [Faith-hardy Christian]
  The confident Christian: seeing with the eyes of faith/Gary L. Harbaugh
  p. cm.
  Originally published: Minneapolis: Augsburg Pub. House, © 1986.
  Includes bibliographical references.
  ISBN 0-8066-4026-X (alk. paper)
  1. Christian life—Lutheran authors. 2. Myers-Briggs Type Indicator.
I. Title.

BV4501.2.H3385 2000
248.4'841—dc21   99-53602

The paper used in this publication meets the minimum requirements of American
National Standard for Information Sciences—Permanence of Paper for Printed
Library Materials, ANSI Z329.48-1984.

Manufactured in the U.S.A.   AF 9-4026

04   03   02   01   00   1   2   3   4   5   6   7   8   9   10

This book is dedicated to my mother and father and those teachers, parishioners, and students whose faith-hardy witness has enriched my life and my faith. Among them are Willard, Marie, T. A., Frances, Luther, David, Jinny, Roy, and Gert, who helped me enter pastoral ministry with courage and confidence not in myself but in Christ. In each parish and classroom that followed, Christ has continued to reveal his presence and care through such persons of faith. I thank God for the special gift that you are to me.

CONTENTS

INTRODUCTION

What does it mean to be a confident Christian? In the Bible, confidence is based on a trusting faith (for example, Abraham with Isaac; Jesus in the Garden of Gethsemane; the disciples courageously overcoming all kinds of opposition to carry out Christ's Great Commission to go into all nations baptizing and teaching). In the development of language, the Latin root of the word *confidence (fides* = faith or trust) reinforces the relationship of confidence and trusting faith, as does the English dictionary when it defines confidence as "belief, faith, reliance, trust." Therefore, with assurance we can say that a confident, faithful Christian is a trusting Christian.

Where does a confident Christian place that trust? Consider two options. Some Christians are confident that they know the way God wants life to be lived and they trust that their good thoughts, words, and deeds as they go about their lives will be rewarded with salvation and eternal life. Regular church attendance and faithfulness in religious practices may increase their confidence as a Christian.

The trouble with confidence that is based on what we do or do not is that at some point we find ourselves in the dilemma of the apostle Paul: "What I do is not the good I want to do; no, the evil I do not want to do—this I keep doing" (Romans 7:19).

All confidence that is based on what we do or do not do is vulnerable to becoming confidence lost! Things change, and we change. In the twinkling of a wandering eye or interpersonal insensitivity or moral lapse or the loosening of an unbridled tongue, today's resolve can become tomorrow's regret. Confidence built on our success at living rightly is a foundation that ever so quickly can be shaken.

Is it possible, then, to be a confident Christian in a changing and challenging world? The biblical answer clearly is yes—if we base our confidence not on what can change, but on the Unchangeable!

A prayer from the *Lutheran Book of Worship* (Minneapolis: Augsburg Publishing House) is very meaningful to me and captures what it means to be a confident Christian:

> Oh, Lord, you have called your servants
> To ventures of which we cannot see the ending,
> By paths as yet untrodden,
> Through perils unknown.
> Give us faith to go out with good courage,
> Not knowing where we go,

But only that your hand is leading us
And your love supporting us,
Through Jesus Christ our Lord.

In this prayer, Christian confidence is the confidence of faith. Not confidence in how much faith we have or how faithful we are, but the confidence of faith in God's hand leading us and God's love supporting us in Christ Jesus our Lord!

Our confidence as a Christian, therefore, is not in ourselves, but in the unchanging presence and care of Christ in a changing and challenging world. Our confidence in Christ gives us hope and courage to deal with life where so often we cannot see the endings and find ourselves on unfamiliar and perilous paths. Our confidence is in Christ's embracing our sin and shortfalls in graceful forgiveness and encouragement to return to God's Way, Truth, and Life.

Confidence in ourselves and our ability to "get right" with God by what we do leads to a relentless striving. Confidence in Christ as Lord and what he has done for us as our Savior leads to a reliant thriving. Reliance on ourselves leads to a rigid adherence to moral law and religious requirements and an anxious faith (because we always fall short of perfection). Reliance on Jesus Christ who loves us so much as to give himself for us and who is present and caring as we face the changes and challenges of life leads to the resilient and transformative and confident faith that I call "faith-hardiness."

FAITH-HARDINESS

There is a personality characteristic that can be called resilience or hardiness. Resilient, hardy individuals seem to be better able to handle life's stresses because of their optimistic outlook and positive approach to life.

I think hardiness helps. But I believe that the kind of hardiness that ultimately helps relies not on our own power but on faith in the power of Christ's presence and caring. That's why I call it "faith-hardiness."
A faith-hardy Christian is able to see the challenges and the choices in times of change because he or she is confident that Christ is present and caring during those times. When Christ walks with us through times of transition, then our eyes are opened to see opportunities and options that otherwise we would overlook.

The confident Christian is a faith-hardy Christian. With Christ as Lord and Savior, our lives are gracefully held in God's hand (Isaiah 49:16 goes so far as to say our very names are engraved on the palms of God's hand!). We are God's own. Our place with God is assured through the death and resurrection of Christ Jesus. There is no need for us to try to find a way to God, for God has given us the Way through Christ. All we do is receive God's gift of the Son and salvation through faith. Then, in gratitude for the gifts of God's love and acceptance and eternal life, we choose to live as a faith-hardy and confident Christian.

This book is meant to help the reader become a more faith-hardy, confident Christian. Confidence and faith-hardiness are so interrelated that at times I will use the terms interchangeably. Faith-hardiness leads to confidence, and confidence is an expression of faith-hardiness. In this book, I will also speak to you as a fellow believer, someone who already knows and trusts in God. If you are like me, however, you probably don't always put into practice what you believe. Like me, you want to be more faithful and effective in living your faith and to become even more confident as a Christian in the midst of the stresses and changes of life.

In this book we will meet some people who are all members of the same Christian congregation. Their problems are not unlike those experienced by many other Christians, perhaps even members of your own church. One of them, whom I refer to as "Joe," was informed by his manager that he was being transferred to another city.* Joe had

---

*Except for the author's references to himself, no name or situation in this book reflects a particular individual, and none should be inferred. The main themes, however, have appeared repeatedly in the author's research, and in that sense the stories are true to life.

gone through a relocation just two years earlier, and he was totally unprepared for another move. He did not know how he could tell his wife, Elaine. They had had such a hard time with their son, Bobby, after the last transfer. But as far as Joe could see, he had little choice. It was either take the transfer or lose his job. Joe was really quite depressed about the whole affair and especially about the way it had been handled by his boss.

George faced a very different type of situation. His heart attack left him unable to do the vigorous construction work that had been a source of satisfaction all his life. While his physician had been encouraging, George wondered if he would ever again look with pride on a house he had built with his own hands.

The downward turn in Kristin's life had taken place much more gradually, even though the final result was a surprise. Kristin and Todd were married at a young age—"too young," her parents had said. As first she and her husband got along quite well, but after the birth of their first child, their marriage began to flounder. Their communication began to slip and with it their intimacy. Kristin was aware that Todd was gone from home more than he had been before. Then one day, after their second child and after ten years of marriage, Todd suddenly announced that he was leaving. At first Kristin was dumbfounded. After she realized Todd was serious, she was determined to make a go of it even though she didn't see how she could. She had a part-time job but no real education or training for good employment.

How would you handle problems like these? Would you approach them in a faith-hardy way or just do your best to get through? Do you see change as a challenge? When things are not going well for you, are you aware of the choices and options you have? Do you see tough times as opportunities to grow as a person and as a Christian? Is faith-hardiness a gift that some have and others do not? Or can Christians grow in faith-hardiness? My message is that faith-hardiness is both a gift and a possibility for all of us. It is a gift because all good things come from God. It is a possibility because our God desires for us all good things and wants us to grow in our use of them.

In order to grow in faith-hardiness, we have to have an idea of how faith-hardy we are now. The first thing you might want to do is take the Faith-Hardiness Inventory. You'll see how faith-hardiness is related to every area of our life as bodily, thinking, feeling, and relating persons. Then, through the use of case studies, we'll take a look at some Christians facing fairly common problems with which most of us will be able to identify. We'll discuss such problems as stress, maintaining control, dealing with loss, handling conflict situations, and finding a meaningful way to express our spirituality. We'll comment on the different ways people approach these issues and what might lie behind some of these patterns. Then we'll look at how these same problems might be dealt with from a faith-hardy perspective. Finally, we'll provide some specific suggestions for your personal growth in faith-hardiness.

Please keep in mind what I said earlier: Faith-hardiness is not a way to God. It is what grows out of our trust in Christ, who is God's way to us. The faith-hardy Christian counts on Christ to be with us always, as he promised he would be. Since God keeps his promises, our calling is to believe them enough to live out their implications in our lives. We do this not to earn God's favor but to show our thankfulness for his grace.

You will find optimism in this book. I am not that optimistic about myself or human nature. But like the apostle Paul, I thank God that sin does not have the final word. We live by the Spirit. Of course, those of us who live by the Spirit are also called to walk by the Spirit (Galatians 5:25). My optimism is in the Christ who not only calls us to live and walk by the Spirit but also promises to walk with us every step of the way. And my confidence is in a Christ who carries us when we are having trouble making it on our own.

I hope this book will help you grow in confidence that every stressful situation can become a challenge and an opportunity to take our next step with courage born of the confidence that God's hand is leading us and God's love supporting us through the presence and care of Christ. That Christ walks before us and with us on our way is the confidence of the faith-hardy Christian.

1

HOW FAITH-HARDY
ARE YOU?

Joe's job transfer, George's illness, and Kristin's marital disruption are problems any one of us could have to face. Is there a way to predict how you might handle such a time of stress in your own life?

Since 1980, more than one thousand Christian laypersons, seminarians, and pastors have taken a questionnaire designed to show how our way of looking at problems affects how we handle them. Most of the ideas came from my research on the whole person and Christian ministry, but some came from studies of psychological "hardiness" by Salvatore R. Maddi and Suzanne C. Kobasa. It is the integration of these ideas that led to my creation of the Faith-Hardiness Inventory.

On page 150 of this book you will find the Faith-Hardiness Inventory, and, if you complete the form, you will get some idea of how faith-hardy you are at this time. Before you complete the Faith-Hardiness Inventory, however, it should be said that there are some limitations to what you are about to do. First the Faith-Hardiness Inventory has been reduced to 20 questions. Perhaps you know an additional area of your life that would be important to consider if you are really to grow in faith-hardiness.

Second, only you can tell how accurate your self-assessment is. There is no validity scale on the Faith-Hardiness Inventory. This means that you could answer the questions the way you would like things to be or the way someone else would like you to answer. You may end up with an "ideal" score but not learn very much about yourself. The only way the Faith-Hardiness Inventory can be of any help to you is if you answer the questions just as honestly as you can. Remember, God already knows you better than you do yourself, and he loves you anyway. There is nothing to lose and perhaps much to gain by "telling it like it is."

Now turn to page 150 and complete the Faith-Hardiness Inventory. Then follow the instructions that are given to find your Faith-hardiness scores.

FAITH-HARDINESS AND WHOLENESS

The Faith-Hardiness Inventory asks you to examine your physical, psychological, and spiritual well-being—to look at yourself as a whole person. As a way of learning what your individual responses to the questions might mean, let's look at each of the following areas of concern to Christians.

PHYSICAL HEALTH

Most Christians who have taken the Faith-Hardiness Inventory indicate that they are generally healthy but are under considerable stress. This says something about our way of life nowadays. It also suggests that it is important to learn and practice some ways of managing our stress if we want to stay healthy.

Where did you rank the physical in comparison with the mental, emotional, and social? Many Christians rank the physical as least important of all, and this is particularly true of clergy. And many do very little to take care of their bodies, at least not on a regular basis. The Faith-Hardiness Inventory is a reminder that our body is a gift, and it is important that we think about how we care for such a good gift from God.

PSYCHOLOGICAL WELL-BEING

Psychological well-being includes both personal and relational wholeness. The mental, emotional, and social dimensions are represented on the

Faith-Hardiness Inventory in a number of ways. Psychological well-being is related to certain attitudes of openness, confidence, and acceptance of limitations.

Every Christian has to struggle with situations of change and loss. Joe and his family were confronted with the loss of family stability, Kristin with the loss of a relationship, George with the loss of health. Faith-hardy Christians are not spared having to deal with these difficult issues. Their grief is as real and their reactions as intense. They wonder why such bad things happen and, at times, become anxious and depressed. What is different about the faith-hardy is that, through it all, they remain hopeful. They believe that, hard as it may be to understand, God is going before them, preparing the way to a more promising tomorrow.

SPIRITUAL WELL-BEING AND INTEGRATION

Spiritual well-being is very much related to the way persons answer the Faith-Hardiness Inventory questions about the physical, mental, emotional, and social dimensions of life. When forced to rank these dimensions along with the spiritual, the faith-hardy usually place the spiritual first. However, as is pointed out in the interpretation of the Faith-Hardiness scores (pages 155–58), the spiritual must not be seen as only a part of life. Rather, as will be graphically shown later, the spiritual is at the center of life.

Though the faith-hardy Christian is religious, the real indication of faith-hardiness is not to be found simply in how many "religious" things the person does. Neither can faith-hardy persons be identified by whether or not they say that Christ is with them in times of trouble. Most Christians say that. The difference is that the faith-hardy *believe* it and have a trusting confidence in Christ's presence and caring. When Christians believe that God actually fulfills his promise to be with us always, this results in a new way of "seeing" and a new way of acting.

Faith-hardy Christians "see" with the eyes of faith. Because Christ is present and caring, any change in our life is also a challenge and an opportunity. If Christ is standing with and under us, how could it be otherwise? And the faith-hardy person believes that in every situation a present and caring Christ calls us to make choices that reflect our new life in him. In other words, there are always choices and options, however limiting the circumstances may be. George did not have a choice about the condition of his heart, but he most certainly had a choice as to how he would deal with his heart condition.

Faith-hardy Christians who let their faith in Christ support them during stressful times of change and loss not only feel better about themselves and life, they also act more effectively and faithfully. This shows up on the Faith-Hardiness Inventory. If your answers were accurate descriptions of your attitudes, feelings, and behaviors, then the more faith-hardy you are (the Faith-Hardiness score), the more likely it is that you also have a positive sense of physical and psychological well-being (the Well-Being score). You are also more likely to go about your life more confidently and hopefully (the Wholeness score). The faith-hardy look to the word of God, baptism, and the Lord's supper as vital supports in their life, and prayer and the Bible are sources of personal strength.

In summary, the faith-hardy man or woman feels better physically and psychologically and is more integrated spiritually. Because the faith-hardy believe that Christ is present and cares for them, they look for and see more choices and options when the going gets rough. Knowing that every changing situation calls us to make the kind of choices that lead to a fuller and more meaningful life, a faith-hardy Christian sees that change is not only a threat, it is also a challenge to grow as a person in Christ.

A HOPEFUL AND HARDY FAITH

What does it mean if you did very poorly on the Faith-Hardiness Inventory? Does that mean that you are not a good Christian? Worse yet, does that mean that your salvation is in question?

These are very good and important questions. Christian theology is very clear that nothing we do, or could do, can earn us a place with God. Sin is real, and the apostle Paul made no exceptions when he said, "All have sinned and fall short of the glory of God" (Romans 3:23). None of us can bring a clean slate to the Lord unless God himself wipes the slate clean.

But there is good news! God has come to us in Christ Jesus and restored us to himself. Our sins have been forgiven. We are acceptable to God because of what he has done for us through Christ our Lord. Our salvation is by grace alone. A hardy faith, then, is not a way to God. A way to God is not possible, nor is it needed since God has come to us.

What we Christians *can* do is to thank God for his gracious love. Becoming more faith-hardy is one way to say that "thank you" to God. Sin continues to cloud our vision and compromise our choices. Our lives at times do not reflect a confident, hardy faith! But, for Jesus' sake, we continue to be forgiven, renewed, and called again to delight in God's will and walk in his ways—to let our faith in Christ make a difference in the way we live our life. A faith-hardy Christian makes a confident witness the world very badly needs.

Understood in this way, your scores on the Faith-Hardiness Inventory have nothing to do with your acceptability to God. But they may be a challenge to you as you grow in confidence as a person in Christ. Your answers to specific questions may also help you to identify where growth might be most desirable if you are to become the most resilient, hardy, confident Christian you can be.

BECOMING MORE FAITH HARDY

Each of the chapters that follows is designed to help you grow in faith-hardiness. We'll take a closer look at the problem of stress and how faith-hardy Christians can turn stressful situations into opportunities for growth. We'll do the same thing with the problem of how to maintain a sense of control when everything around us is changing, how to lose gracefully, and how to fight fairly and faithfully. These are tough problems for Christians, but the faith-hardy Christian knows that they are not too tough when the Lord is with us.

How might you get the most out of reading this book? Some people like to get an overall impression, have a lot to think about, and then apply what they have learned to their lives. If you are like that, you may want to start at the beginning of this book and read right through to the end, returning to the specific chapter suggestions only after you finish reading.

Rather than reading through the book in one sitting, it might be more helpful to read one chapter at a time. Each of the chapters is a complete unit in itself, with a particular problem, a discussion of the issues involved, and specific suggestions to consider putting into practice.

While you can gain a lot by reading alone, there are benefits in getting a few of your friends to read the book at the same time and then coming together to discuss it. A supportive group like this can give you feedback on what could be most helpful for you, in your situation, to try out first. Support groups can also help you keep your motivation for growth high and strong. Most importantly, support groups can be a way for Christ to fulfill his promise to be with us in a caring, comforting, and challenging way.

2

PUTTING STRESS
IN ITS PLACE

Stress is as much of a problem for Christians as for anyone else. But stress is also an opportunity to know oneself better and to become more whole. It is a challenge for us to grow as persons in Christ. The reactions of Kristin and Elaine to the changes in their lives will help us get a better idea of how a faith-hardy perspective can help us put stress in its proper place.

When her husband left, the bottom of Kristin's world seemed to drop out. She blamed herself. She wondered if it was because she had gained so much weight or maybe because she didn't like Todd's friends. At first Kristin didn't want anyone to know, not even her parents. She had never talked very much with others about herself. She was a warm person but rather shy. Only one coworker at the place where Kristin worked part-time had any idea that something had happened, but Kristin avoided any real conversation with her. She was also embarrassed to go to church. For the preceding two years she had helped out with the preschool children during Sunday school—in part because she had a preschooler but also because she liked children. She wondered what the parents of the children in her class would think if they knew.

One of the problems that had plagued Kristin's marriage was her difficulty with setting limits. She just couldn't seem to say no, even when she knew that she needed to. She would try to resist being taken advantage of, but in the end she would give in, swallowing her feelings. Todd played that for all he could, leaving most of the childcare to her and, after a time, even insisting that she look for a job. Todd's hobby was cars, and that was expensive. It also took him away on many weekends, going to car shows or attending his mechanic's group. On one of those weekends he met another woman, and soon he was gone for good. Kristin was hurt by this rejection, but she was as anxious as she was depressed. She was terribly concerned about how she would support her young family.

Elaine also faced an unexpected change. On the day Joe learned about his transfer, when he pulled into the driveway and started toward his house, Elaine met him at the door. She was smiling. "Wait until you hear about Bobby's school assignment for next year," she said.

"Elaine," Joe interrupted. He could hardly look her in the eye. "The main office called me at work today, and—"

"Oh, no!" Elaine said, "Not another move!"

Joe and Elaine had been transferred only two years ago and were just now really feeling adjusted to their new community. The church had come to mean a great deal to them, especially after the pastor helped them with Bobby. For a while Joe and Elaine talked about what another move would mean, especially to their son. Their emotions were raw and, at times, more heat than light was shed on the situation.

After a time Elaine said, "OK. Let's see what we can do with this. Things may not be as bad as they seem. Right now I need to get rid of some of this tension. Let's go for our walk." Elaine had read about the benefits of exercise and walking and had persuaded Joe that it would be good for them to do several times a week. They walked especially fast that evening.

As they walked they were silent. Elaine's thoughts kept turning to her parents. Her father and mother were dead now, but Elaine always remembered how her father had handled the diagnosis of his terminal cancer. He had been determined to make the best of it and live fully until it was time to die. Her father's faith had been a source of great strength for him, as it had been for her mother after his death. Elaine thought to herself that the news of another move was something like a death. It certainly felt like it. How might she let her faith help her through this time as it had helped her father?

One thing Elaine knew for certain was that she wanted to talk the problem over with the members of her women's group. While she wanted support from them, she also wanted something more. A number of the women in the group had moved around quite a bit, too. She knew they would be helpful. Elaine remembered one of the first sermons she had heard the pastor preach. It was on the importance of how people handle turning points in their lives. At the time she heard it Elaine had thought about her father but most about her son and their recent relocation. She had hoped there wouldn't be another situation like that too soon. But here it was. Maybe the pastor would have some suggestions.

WHO HANDLES
STRESS WELL, AND WHY

Major transitions in life are usually very stressful. Two physicians have shown us just how difficult change can be. Perhaps you have seen the widely used stress scale developed by Drs. Thomas Holmes and Richard Rahe (see opposite page).

On this scale, every item is given a certain number of life change units (LCU). A total score

Rank	Life Event	LCU	Rank	Life Event	LCU
1	Death of spouse	119	23	Mortgage/loan greater than $10,000	44
2	Divorce	98	24	Change in responsibilities at work	43
3	Death of close family member	92	25	Change in living conditions	42
4	Marital separation	79	26	Change in residence	41
5	Fired from work	79	27	Begin or end school	38
6	Major personal injury or illness	77	28	Trouble with in-laws	38
7	Jail term	75	29	Outstanding personal achievement	37
8	Death of close friend	70	30	Change in work hours or conditions	36
9	Pregnancy	66	31	Change in schools	35
10	Major business readjustment	62	32	Christmas	30
11	Foreclosure on a mortgage or loan	61	33	Trouble with boss	29
12	Gain of new family member	57	34	Change in recreation	29
13	Marital reconciliation	57	35	Mortgage/loan less than $10,000	28
14	Change of health/behavior of family member	56	36	Change in personal habits	27
15	Change in financial state	56	37	Change in eating habits	27
16	Retirement	54	38	Change in social activities	27
17	Change to different line of work	51	39	Change in number of family get-togethers	26
18	Change in number of arguments with spouse	51	40	Change in sleeping habits	26
19	Marriage	50	41	Vacation	25
20	Spouse begins or ends work	46	42	Change in church activities	22
21	Sexual difficulties	45	43	Minor violation of the law	22
22	Child leaving home	44			

The Holmes-Rahe Social Readjustment Scale

of more than 300 in any one calendar year can mean a person has a greater susceptibility to physical or emotional problems, and a score of 450 or more makes the likelihood of some kind of illness about 80 percent higher! If you mark the items that Kristin's or anyone's marital estrangement and divorce usually involve, you will see how quickly the score gets to 300, and maybe much more.

What is so difficult about change? If you think about it, any major change involves a loss of some kind or another. The loss is obvious when the change is the result of a marital dissolution or the death of a loved one. The loss may be less obvious, but every bit as real, when a job description or location is altered or when people no longer are physically able to go about life in their usual way.

Remember, too much change in too short a time leaves a person vulnerable. Physical or mental health can suffer. In other words, stress is serious business.

Another look at the Holmes-Rahe scale makes it clear that everyone has some degree of stress to deal with. It is not at all unusual for a person to accumulate quite a number of LCUs on the stress scale. A realistic goal is not to eliminate stress from life but to handle it more effectively.

Who handles stress best, and why? There are different answers to this question. Some say that the most effective way to put stress in its place is by practicing good physical self-care. Others say that the main factor is having an active social emotional support group. Still others suggest that certain personality characteristics make stress more manageable. Let's look at these approaches to see what they have to offer.

SELF-CARE

Books on stress ordinarily suggest that a good self-care program is very important if a person is not to become a stress casualty. Usually some form of physical exercise is prescribed, such as jogging or the fast walking that Elaine read about. The most helpful physical workout not only develops good muscle tone but also exercises the heart and lungs. Of course, a prior visit to a physician is important to make certain that your plans for self-care don't do unintended harm to your body. But once they have medical clearance, those who regularly jog or fast walk report that their physical workout is one effective way to combat stress.

Self-care also refers to such things as healthy nutrition, various types of relaxation exercises, and the use of such techniques as biofeedback and self-hypnotism. Nutrition is related to the amount of physical and mental energy we have at our disposal to handle the problems of living. Sometimes very grand claims are made about the benefits of eating a certain way or taking particular dietary supplements. I do not know what the truth is about these various claims, but there is no question in my mind that I function more effectively when I eat regular and nutritious meals. On occasion I have not had time for breakfast and something occurs that also keeps me from eating lunch. By mid-afternoon my body is sending out distress signals and my mind has slowed down considerably. However, just eating is not the message of nutritionists. *What* is eaten is even more important. Of course, just as with exercise, it is good to check with a physician before making a major change in your way of nourishing your body.

As an alternative to drugs or sometimes in combination with appropriately prescribed medications, relaxation exercises, including different approaches to meditation and self-hypnotism, seem to help some persons reduce feelings of stress. Biofeedback usually involves teaching a patient one of the relaxation techniques and then monitoring the progress of that individual with mechanical methods such as a temperature gauge or muscle tension indicator. The body seems to warm when relaxed and, obviously, muscles are less tense.

I think good self-care makes a lot of sense. A healthy diet can go a long way toward our feeling better and handling day-to-day stresses more confidently. Keeping our intake of alcohol and other chemicals to a minimum also should enhance both our physical functioning and our sense of being able to handle our life situation. Properly prescribed physical exercises and other stress-reducing techniques are effective in making the stress we experience more manageable and less immediately harmful.

During the peak of the stress of her estrangement and divorce, it would be very understandable that Kristin might not take care of herself as well as she might under other circumstances. Emotional distress can affect both appetite and the motivation to start or keep up with physical self-care. It is also possible that the children may not have their nutritional needs met as well as before, especially if Kristin is unable to be at home as much or if she has difficulty finding the right person to stay with her children when she is gone. But it may be more important than ever for Kristin to pay attention to these basic needs of herself and her family. Her ability to withstand the pressures of this period will be increased if she does.

SOCIAL SUPPORT

A second reason why some persons handle stress better than others depends on how good their social support system is. How *good* does not necessarily mean how *large*. A person could have many friends, but they might not be very sympathetic or understanding. They may not listen very well. They may be eager to provide answers before they have really heard the deeper questions.

Or a group may be *too* sympathetic and understanding, in an unhealthy sense. If Kristin were to join such a group, her feelings of help-lessness and hopelessness could be increased if all she heard was how bad her situation was and how other deserted wives and children had never fully recovered from their rejection and abandonment.

A good social support system, such as Elaine had, is composed of warm and caring family and friends who listen without judgment. But more than listening is involved in the kind of support systems that help reduce stress. There needs to be both the opportunity to share deep and uncomfortable feelings and to share constructive suggestions for making the situation more manageable. The key is the timing. Jumping right to problem solving can cause a hurting person to feel unheard and uncared about. Never getting to problem solving can turn a potential social support group into nothing other than a series of gripe sessions.

Social support frameworks can exist on the job, in the home, and in the congregation. Ideally they are found in each of these places. But even if they exist, we have to be willing to use them. When

Todd announced he was leaving, Kristin started cutting herself off from any potential sources of support. She began to avoid the one coworker who showed some awareness of her having a hard time. She stayed home from church, feeling guilty and uncomfortable about being around "good" people, a category she thought no longer included her. She was uncertain how her parents would react, so she did not risk talking with them.

The simple truth is that we need each other. More than ever, we need each other in times of stress. What that means may be different for different people, but the bottom line is that we need to know that we are cared about as we are. Until others know *where* we are and *how* we are, they cannot really care about us *as* we are. One of the greatest blessings of life and greatest buffers against the stressful changes of life is to have family and friends who will be there for us where we are, really listen to how we are, and love us as we are.

PERSONALITY

"As we are" has to do with our personality, and personality has a lot to do with the way we handle stress. There are two perspectives on personality that I think are especially important.

PERSONALITY TYPES AND STRESS

All people experience some stress, regardless of their personality type, because life involves change, and change is stressful. However, what feels most stressful to one person may not be what stresses someone else. Part of the reason for that is the difference in personality types.

One of the most helpful ways to understand our personality type is to take the Myers-Briggs Type Indicator®, or MBTI®. The MBTI® results indicate what our basic preferences are and what they mean. No one type is "better" than another. Each type has certain strengths and certain limitations.

For example, are you more oriented toward the outer world of people and things or are you more oriented toward the inner world of thoughts and ideas? When your energy is not depleted, but a little low, do you like to be around people to get charged up again—or do you get your energy renewed by getting off by yourself, maybe reading a book or meditating? The more outgoing person is acting more extraverted, the other more introverted. Of course, everyone likes to be with others sometimes and likes to be alone at other times. Personality type has to do with what most of the time we naturally *prefer,* which may not be what our life situation requires us actually to do.

In addition to extraversion and introversion, each of us also has a basic, probably inborn, preference for a certain way of seeing the world and making decisions about what we see. You may pay close attention to what is going on in the here and now. You keep your eyes and ears open for facts and details. Others might be more future-oriented. They use their senses, too, but quickly jump to what the facts mean and how individual details are related to each other in larger patterns of meaning.

Once we "see" what we see (present facts or future possibilities), we have to decide what to do. People may use logic and impersonal analysis to make decisions, which they would like to be as objective as possible. Another way to make decisions is to consider what is important to ourselves and to others and to decide what to do on the basis of our personal, subjective values.

Finally, people prefer different ways of living from day to day. Some prefer to live a planned, orderly way of life and they very much like to be in control of their life situation. Others prefer to live a flexible and spontaneous way, without any more prior planning than absolutely necessary. The first personality life-style preference values punctuality and schedules, even when they are not required by others. The second personality life-style preference adapts very naturally to changing circumstances and the calendar is rarely in concrete.

Research studies suggest that certain Myers-Briggs® personality types are more vulnerable to some kinds of stress. Elaine is more extraverted than Kristin, which is shown by her active involvement with women's groups and especially by her ease in taking the initiative in social relationships. Kristin, on the other hand, tends to stay more to herself and values thinking things through by herself. Ordinarily it is not a problem for her to be by herself. But when a situation arises which is more than what most people can handle on their own, then the introvert may be at a disadvantage. While there are other ways in which the MBTI® can be helpful in our understanding of stress, including what stresses us and why, at this point I simply want to emphasize that the personality of the individual who has to deal with change plays a part in how stressed that person feels.

THE HARDY PERSONALITY

Another perspective that is very important when it comes to understanding stress is what Maddi and Kobasa call hardiness. The hardy personality is invested and involved in life, eager to take the challenges that life offers, and confident that he or she can influence the outcome of even a very difficult situation. In other words, hardiness is marked by the characteristics of commitment, challenge, and control. The hardy person tends to be optimistic, ingenious, enterprising, decisive, and action-oriented.

Hardiness has about it the feel of competence, mastery, and achievement.

Kristin is not psychologically very hardy. When Kristin learned that Todd was going to leave, she pulled away from others and into herself. Most of her thoughts were negative and self-protective. She was understandably worried about the well-being of her family, but unfortunately she felt that she was in the grip of forces that were completely beyond her control. She thought there was nothing she could do and that there was not much hope for anything good coming out of the situation.

Elaine was not any happier than Kristin was to hear the news about the coming change in her life. She really liked living where she did and had hoped to remain there much longer. Her first response was a kind of denial, half hopeful that she wasn't hearing what Joe was saying. It is important to remember that hardy people feel the same things that the less hardy feel. The difference is in what the hardy *do*. As soon as Elaine caught her breath, she moved beyond her own feelings and asked Joe what *he* was feeling. For a while, Joe and Elaine talked about what a move would mean, especially to Bobby. But Elaine did not allow her feelings to overwhelm her. She was determined to do what she could to make the situation better.

I believe that psychological hardiness is very desirable to have. Research shows that hardy people are much less likely to become stress casualties. Psychological hardiness is especially helpful when people are in a situation that, with a little imagination and effort, can be changed for the better.

Why do some people handle stress better than others? We have seen that there are a number of answers to that question. First, self-care helps. Second, a good social-support system can mean a lot. Finally, both the perspective of personality type and personality hardiness show that personality plays an important role in how people perceive their situation and what they can do about it.

WHAT ARE YOUR WAYS OF HANDLING STRESS?

Let's now take a look at how the Faith-Hardiness Inventory helps you to evaluate what you are doing about the stress in your life. First, take a few moments to review your answers to the following questions on the Faith-Hardiness Inventory:

At what level would you assess your physical health at the present time?

		very
excellent	1 2 3 4 5	poor

With *all* factors considered (personal and family relationships, work, health, finances, etc.), if you were to take a stress test covering the past year, where do you think you would score?

| very
calm
and relaxed | 1 2 3 4 5 | very
highly
stressed |

Regardless of the number of stressful events they experience, people are different in how stressed they subjectively *feel*. Generally speaking, are you:

| very
calm
and relaxed | 1 2 3 4 5 | very
highly
stressed |

A common way many persons try to manage stress in their lives is by doing things to take care of themselves. Such self-care often involves an attempt to balance life with time for adequate rest, relaxation, exercise, nutrition, personal growth activities, etc. Taking into account both how much you know about self-care *and* how well you practice it, at what level would you rate your self-care at the present time?

| informed
and
skilled | 1 2 3 4 5 | uninformed
and
unskilled |

Now check any of the following forms of self-care that you *regularly* practice:

___ physical exercise, jogging, fast walk-ing, etc.
___ balanced nutrition
___ relaxation techniques, biofeedback, etc.
___ time management (prioritize, limit hours, time off)
___ self-help reading
___ personal support group(s)
___ regular personal Bible reading
___ personal prayer and other private devotions
___ worship and other corporate reli-gious practices
___ other _____

When you are in a stressful situation, how do you *usually* perceive change?

a challenge and an opportunity	1 2 3 4 5	an obstacle or a danger

Your answers on the Faith-Hardiness Inventory will give you some idea of what your approach to stress is. There are questions about self-care, your use of social support, and your personality preferences.

How good is your self-care? What do you do *regularly* to take care of yourself? You rated your level of self-care. How consistent is that estimate with what you actually do to feel at your best? Do you practice one form of self-care or many? Are there things you *used* to do but don't do any longer? Why? Is there anything you would like to do but haven't gotten around to yet?

How much you rely on a social-support system can show up in several places on the inventory. One place is whether or not you are a part of any personal support groups or if you perceive your congregational experience as supportive. Another is how you filled in the "other" self-care line. If you did not say that you were part of a support group, did you write in something that suggests you consider interpersonal relationships as an important form of self-care? If you did neither, then you might want to consider whether or not you have adequately developed a social-support system that you can call on in times of stressful change.

Your personality shows up not only in the question about how you usually perceive change, as a challenge or a danger, but also in the types of self-care that you practice. Are your self-care preferences more outgoing and extraverted, such as participating in a support group or an exercise group? Or are they more individual and introverted, such as a relaxation exercise you do alone or self-help reading? Do you select things to do that require organization, repetition, and discipline? Or do you like to adapt the type of self-care you practice to whatever the immediate situation requires?

The reason I want to emphasize the importance of the combination of self-care, social support, and personality in your handling of stress is that I believe a (w)holistic approach is both more faithful and it has the best chance of working. That's why being faith-hardy helps.

FAITH-HARDINESS AND WHOLENESS

My understanding of faith-hardiness is based on a biblical model of wholeness that includes the physical, mental, emotional, and social dimensions of life. One way to see how all these "parts" of being human interrelate and interact is by arranging the dimensions like this:

A Biblical Model of Wholeness

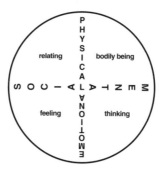

(W)holistic Model

A Biblical Model of Wholeness is copyright © Gary L. Harbaugh , Ph.D.

In the Faith-Hardiness Inventory, you were asked to rank the physical, mental, emotional, and social dimensions, along with the spiritual, in the order of their importance to you. You may have had a hard time doing that. The fact is that to live well we can't neglect *any* "part" of us. We need to attend to our body, use our mind, be in touch with our feelings, and meaningfully relate to others if we are to be healthy and whole persons.

The reason we cannot neglect a "part" of us and still be whole is that, biblically, every "part" of a person represents the whole person. The creation story doesn't just talk about people *getting* a new part, called a "soul." Actually the Hebrew word for soul, *nephesh,* means "a living being." By God's creative act people *become* souls— living beings. Sometimes we think of the heart as being a part of us, but when the psalmist talks about repentance bringing about a "new" or a "clean" heart, what is meant is that the whole person is renewed. So when the words *soul* or *heart* are used in the Bible, we need to think about the whole person.

The Old Testament and New Testament understanding of what it means to be a person are the same, and Jesus' teaching makes it clear that we are whole persons before God. To love God with all our heart, soul, mind, and strength is to respond to God with all that we are.

"All that we are" includes our relationships with each other. In the Bible, the response of a person to God is never a totally private affair. Any one person's response is linked with the human community. To have peace *(shalom)* is therefore to be in a right relationship with oneself, one's neighbor, and one's God. This is *life*—the whole person in responsible relationship with self, others, and God. According to the Bible, anything short of *shalom* is not really living.

By arranging the physical, mental, emotional, and social dimensions in such a way as to meet in the center with a common "L," this model of wholeness is a reminder that what happens in any one area of your life will affect every other area. However you ranked the importance of the body, mind, feelings, or relationships, you cannot really separate them as if they had nothing to do with one another. How a person thinks (mentally) and feels (physically and emotionally) is connected with the way that person relates and acts. If you value your intellect, you will think better if you do not neglect your physical needs. If you value your relationships, you will relate better if you are in touch with your feelings. Your way of ranking these dimensions may be a sign of where you need to pay a little more attention if you want to be as healthy as possible and more whole.

Undoubtedly you are wondering where the spiritual fits in. Many Christians rank the spiritual as number one or number two. But where does it fit into a model of wholeness? In this model the spiritual should not be just another "spoke" on the wheel. Christians know that the spiritual dimension is not a part of life but rather at the *heart* of life, at the center of everything.

I show the spiritual by using the center "L" not only as a sign that the physical, mental, emotional, and social areas are interrelated, but also in a deeper and more significant way. The center "L" stands for the integration of all these dimensions in our relationship with God.

In the Bible, "El" is one of the names for God. Placing an "L" at the center of this model is my way of saying that the spiritual is *always* involved in anything that affects our body, mind, feelings, or relationships. The spiritual is not just something we take care of on Sunday morning at church services. True spirituality involves the way we care for physical needs, the way we develop our intellect, the way we strengthen our capacity to feel for and feel with others, and the way we respond to others.

Using a model like this can be helpful to Christians who want to grow in faith-hardiness. Here are three ways to use it:

Think about yourself in relation to the model. Which of the areas are you most likely to overlook as you go about your day-to-day living? A faith-hardy and healthy approach to life is a balanced approach. When I spend too much time with my work and my studies, I neglect my body and my relationships. If that happens too often or for too long, my physical and relational health suffers. I cannot be truly faithful (spiritual) if I do not take care of the temple the Bible says my body is and the family my God has given me to nurture. Looking at the model of wholeness can help us see whether or not our life is in balance. Being out of balance can lead to feeling stressed.

How does a faith-hardy sense of yourself as a whole person help when it comes to handling stress? When we realize that God has created us as bodily persons who are also thinking, feeling, and relating persons, then any form of adequate stress management must touch on all those dimensions of our life: physical, mental, emotional, and social. Many of the methods suggested in books and magazines are not as helpful as they could be because they speak to only one part of us as human beings. Good nutrition, jogging, fast walking, and other physical exercise are all potentially valuable ways to handle stress. But stress is more than a physical reaction, so more than a physical response is needed. If a person's stress is coming from faulty interpersonal relationships, an exercise class may be a preferred way to *reduce* that stress, but exercising will not eliminate the *source* of the stress.

When our way of handling stress does not keep in mind the fact that we are a whole person, then our method often fails us, and in time we give it up. I think this is what lies behind the fact that the vast majority of those who start a self-care routine backslide to their old ways within the short space of six months!

While faith-hardy stress management requires that we do something that will reduce stress in each "part" of our life, it is important to remember that not all stress is to be managed. Sometimes the fact that we are being stressed is a painful reminder that our life is badly out of balance because God is not at the center. At those times the challenge is not simply to *reduce* our stress to a manageable level but to *learn* from it. The best faith-hardy method for *stress prevention* is to remember what it means to be whole persons called to live our lives in responsible relation to God and others.

The social area on the model reminds us that faith-hardy Christians know they need others and others need them. That's the way God made us. When we think that we should be able to handle all our problems on our own, or that our problems are only our own business, then we are forgetting that we in the body of Christ, the church, are members one of another.

Think about the special needs of others. For example, if there has been a death or a loss in one of the families in your congregation, such as when George became ill or when Kristin's husband left, the model could have reminded members of the congregation not to forget the basic needs we have all the time but especially in a time of crisis. Not only are there physical needs, but also the need to talk about what happened (mental) and to express feelings (emotional). When fellow members are in the hospital or convalescing at home, there is a need for visitation (social).

Of course, some ways of being with each other in the church are more faith-hardy than others. We need to grow in our ability to listen to each other. The next time someone begins to share a concern with you, see what happens if you really try to understand how things look to that person. By being a friend to someone in a time of need, you may make a friend who can be there for you when you need someone yourself. The faith-hardy remind themselves that, just as breathing in and out is a rhythm that sustains our body, so giving to and receiving from others is a rhythm God has built into the church as the body of Christ.

A third way to let the model help us grow in faith-hardiness is to let it prompt us to raise the right questions. The integrating "L" reminds us not to overlook the spiritual implications of what we are doing with our body, mind, feelings, family, and friends. Does the way we care for the physical and material needs of ourselves (and others) reflect our faith? Does not only what we say but also how we say it adequately express our relationship to Christ? Emotionally, are we rejoicing with those who rejoice and weeping with those who weep, as the apostle Paul calls us to do? Relationally, are we so wrapped up in what we are doing personally that we are forgetting that we are called into community? If we let the model of wholeness remind us that there are faith implications to every ordinary thing we do, then the model can be a spiritual guide for a more faith-hardy expression of our commitment to Christ.

This spiritual grounding is what distinguishes faith-hardiness from psychological hardiness. To handle stressful times, the psychologically hardy transform stressful events into challenges and, only if all else fails, accept what cannot be changed. To do this, psychological hardiness depends on "some power"—the power of the hardy personality. But psychological hardiness has some limitations. There are times when we are in situations where we can and should take charge. But sometimes in life the real gift is not even to *try* to be in control, but to be able, fully and freely, to let go. Letting go, without any reservations, may be more difficult for those who identify strength with being on top of things whenever possible. Such persons may not fully understand what the apostle Paul meant when he said, "When I am weak, then I am strong" (2 Corinthians 12:10).

I agree that "some power" is needed in the tough times of life, and having a hardy personality helps. But I do not believe that hardiness is adequate if it is only psychological. Something more and deeper is needed. When Elaine's father was dying of cancer, he fought a hard fight, but there came a time when his strength was insufficient. Death is the ultimate challenge for the hardy personality because it strips away our strength and shatters our solutions. Death is not a problem to be solved like other problems in life. It is a reality to be encountered.

Psychological hardiness does help people to change the things that they can change. Believing they have explored every available option, hardiness may even help some people accept with serenity the things they *cannot* change. But psychological hardiness faces its greatest challenge when it comes to the fact of death, because there is no personal power in hardiness that survives the reality of death. Anglican or atheist, Disciple of Christ or disciple of Lao-tzu, Roman Catholic or Russian Communist, each can be as hardy as the other. Death comes to each and all.

Psychological hardiness may say yes to life in the face of death, but this kind of hardiness cannot say yes to death in the name of eternal life. The only yes that embraces life and transcends death is God's yes to us in Jesus Christ (2 Corinthians 1:20). When hardiness comes not out of our personal power but out of Christ's presence and care in our lives, then we are hardy indeed—faith-hardy. Then we know that nothing can separate us from the love of God in Christ Jesus—nothing in life, and not even death!

Because faith-hardiness looks to Christ Jesus for ultimate help and healing, the faith-hardy listen for his voice during times of change and tension. We have already referred to the way that bodily symptoms can help us hear a word from our Lord. God also speaks to us in response to our prayers. But probably the most usual way for us to hear God's word is through another person. For Kristin, it could have been a family member or a friend, but it turned out to have been her pastor. Kristin had never talked with her pastor about her relationship with Todd. However, the pastor was aware that Todd seldom accompanied Kristin to church and that he was increasingly out of town on weekends. When Kristin called in to the Sunday school three Sundays in a row requesting a substitute, her pastor decided to stop by her home to see whether anything was wrong. Kristin was hesitant initially, but soon the whole story came out, with many tears. She acknowledged her humiliation and her fear of what others would say. Most of all she wondered how she would support her children.

The pastor didn't come up with any immediate solutions, but Kristin felt she had been truly heard, and she no longer felt so alone. Something the pastor said toward the end of the visit really helped her turn the corner: "Kristin, my coming to you seems to have helped. I want you to know I didn't come as much as I was sent. Several times I was about to do something else, but I couldn't get you off my mind. I believe our Lord wants you to know that he cares, and that's why I'm here. I'll do whatever I can to help, and I know some others in church who'll want to do what they can, too."

Because someone important to her had listened without judgment, Kristin was encouraged to risk telling her parents and a few of her close friends. When they rallied to her support, Kristin began for the first time to believe that she would be able to make it.

A faith-hardy confidence in the presence of Christ during tough and stressful times keeps us open to the choices that are always around us. Kristin saw, through the confidence she gained in talking with her pastor, that she could continue to try to go it alone, or she could risk letting others know. She had been making a choice that closed herself off from others. Through the pastor, Christ entered her situation in a personal way and gave her the courage to risk. Long ago, Moses reminded the people of God that, especially at the crossroads, we are confronted with curse and blessing, death and life (Deuteronomy 30:19). Our calling is to choose life. Kristin's willingness to look up and reach out was a choice for life.

SUGGESTIONS FOR DEALING WITH STRESS

Let your faith make a difference. Since stress is a fact of modern life, you cannot hope to avoid it. But research has shown that not everybody feels equally stressed, even though they may be in exactly the same situation. Much of it depends on what we "see." To become more faith-hardy, it will be important to ask yourself whether or not, when you are in a stressful situation, you are letting Christ's presence with you make any difference. There is no question that Christ is present—that is his promise. The only question is whether or not you are allowing yourself to feel his presence.

Keep your perspective. Most of the time, what we consider to be stressful is not life-threatening. Much of the time, a year or two from now we won't even remember what bothers us so at this moment. Someone has said that about 80 percent of what we worry about never even comes to pass. Remembering that Christ is present and that he cares can help us not become overanxious about things that do not ultimately matter. After all, if we are his and he is with us (and those we love), we have everything. The apostle Paul said, "If God is for us, who can be against us? . . . Who shall separate us from the love of Christ?" (Romans 8:31, 35). Even when the danger *is* life-threatening, we have God's promise that "whether we live or die, we belong to the Lord" (Romans 14:8).

Nourish your faith. To grow in faith-hardiness, we need to put ourselves in positions where we can hear Christ's promise that he is with us always. When you go to church, listen to the reading of Scripture and follow the words of the hymns so you can absorb the promises through your senses. A good sermon will be filled with the many promises of God, and even a poor sermon usually has more of them than you might realize. Remember, another promise is that God's word accomplishes God's purpose.

Put your faith into practice. After listening for God's promise to be present and caring in your life as a bodily person, then let what you hear have a greater effect on how you live your life. Decide to *act* on your faith in at least one important area of your physical/material life. For example, you may have a program for your financial security during retirement. Perhaps you could take just 10 percent of one month's contribution to that pension plan and commit it to a church world hunger program. That could be a token of your confidence that God will take care of your needs and a way for him, through you, to take care of those who are in need right now.

Learn at least one stress management technique or commit yourself to practice more regularly the self-care approach you already know. To make it more likely that you will not be one of the "dropouts," do something that strengthens you as a whole person—body, mind, feelings, and relating ability.

Do something for others. Whatever you do to take care of yourself, see it as one of the ways that God is helping you to be free from immobilizing stress so you can be freer for ministry. That's the desirable outcome. After calling us, God wants to *use* us so others can be a part of his kingdom. Physical faith-hardiness can be one way that frees us to reach as many others as possible. When I feel good physically, I am less likely to decline a pastor's invitation to make an evening call on a prospective member of the congregation. In other words, my physical self-care is a part of my witness as a hardy Christian. It is one of the ways God fulfills his promises to others through me.

Remember the challenge of stress. The real challenge of stress is not simply to regain control of part of your life. If you see stress only as an annoying problem, then you'll just do whatever it takes to get rid of it. But stress can be God's way of telling us that our lives are unbalanced. We may be feeling tension because our priorities are out of order, and God has been squeezed out of the center of our lives. If we put our energy into reducing or managing stress, then we may miss the chance to learn from it. Faith-hardy Christians are not only interested in stress management but also in the way stress relates to deeper questions of life and faith. If we pay attention to these deeper meanings, we come closer to putting stress in its proper place.

3

How to Be in
Charge and in
Christ

How do we work out in our lives the important balance of holding on and letting go? Kristin had to deal with abandonment. George had a different problem. His story will help us see that being in charge is related to our being in Christ.

George was a big man who loved to work with his hands. None of the other men on his construction crew could keep up with him when he was working at his best, and he always tried to work at his best. People looked up to him not only because of his size, but because he commanded their respect. In a day when true craftsmen are hard to find, George was a living reminder that there are still those who take pride in what they do and how they do it. He knew how houses should be built, and he was determined to build them that way. His construction plans were very precise, and he insisted that they be followed exactly. That's why people in the community were quick to point out if their house had been built by him.

Now George, so full of life and vitality, had been brought to his knees. It happened on a day that started out with happy memories and high expectations. George's son, Stephen, and his family had been home for a visit. Father and son decided to go fishing just as they had when Stephen was a boy growing up. They were even going to take the grandson but decided not to when he came down with a cold. After an exciting day marked by great catches and even more fantastic near-catches, it was time to head back to the shore. Stephen fiddled with the engine a minute and started the motor. The sound covered George's cry of pain as the first contraction hit him. When Stephen turned around to the bow, all he saw was his father's ashen face. The distance from the middle of the lake to the dock had never seemed so far. With a sigh of relief Stephen saw that the bait store was still open. There was a phone there. The ambulance came as fast as it could, which seemed much too long.

George survived, but that was the only good news. The damage to his heart was severe. George would no longer be able to handle the heavier parts of the construction work that he loved so much without risking another, possibly fatal, attack. George wondered what he would do. He no longer felt in charge of his life. He had always said that he would never ask someone else to do what he could not do himself. How could he admit to his crew that he was no longer on top of the work situation?

WHY DO PEOPLE NEED TO BE "ON TOP"?

GROWING UP IN AMERICA

Americans may love the underdog, but what we want is for the underdog to come out on top. Our society recognizes and honors those who succeed much more than we honor those who try hard but fail. So our school teachers prepare young people for such a society by emphasizing performance, and some youth find the pressure so great that school is one big headache. Some coaches drive young men and women to near exhaustion because athletic events are not for fun, they are for winning. Those who come out on top are "OK," and everyone wants to be OK.

Studies of how people grow from infancy to adulthood show that our culture not only affects our public schools, but also our child-rearing practices. When the competition that fills a parent's workday filters into the home, the basic message to a child is that he or she better measure up. When one child is compared to another child or our children are compared to the neighbor's children, then the word our youngsters "hear" is that it is not enough to be themselves. They are not acceptable as they are. Love is conditional.

Psychologists have pointed out that many problems in later adult life are produced by our obsession with coming out on top. The pain of perfectionism is that, no matter how well a perfectionist does, it is never quite good enough. Fortunately, not all persons are so marred by their early training that they become perfectionists—hard on others and even harder on themselves. But many who are not perfectionists still never quite get over the vague feeling that they in some way are inadequate and unlovable unless they change. They just don't quite measure up.

PERSONALITY AND CONTROL

In addition to our cultural bias toward being in charge, some people have a natural personality type that leads them to value an orderly, organized life-style in which they feel that things are under control. The Myers-Briggs Type Indicator® calls such personalities the "J" type. The "J" stands for judging, but it means decisive rather than judgmental. George is an example of someone who has the characteristics of a J personality.

J-type personalities are in the majority in our country. The gifts of the J personality are many. George is not likely to put off until tomorrow the decisions that need to be made today. He is able to plan ahead and, once the direction is set, he has the sustaining power to "stay the course."

There are, however, some limitations to the J personality preference. When the unexpected pops up, when change is required, when what has been counted on no longer is able to be counted on, when adaptability is needed, then the person with a J personality preference may be at a disadvantage. The change may not so much be seen as an opportunity but as a threat to a valued way of living and to personal security.

When persons have a natural need to be in control and, as children, their parents and schools emphasize the importance of their being on top of things, it is more understandable how hard it is for some people to "let go" as they get older. Yet that is exactly what George needed to be able to do. To continue to try to be the example for his crew by outworking them would very likely cost him his life.

"TAKE CHARGE" SITUATIONS

As if it were not enough that our social system encourages coming out on top and many people have personality needs to be in control, there are also some life situations that make it hard to let go. For example, when Kristin was deserted by her husband, she was the only responsible adult left to take care of her family. Whether she had a J personality or not, Kristin had to take charge if she and her children were going to survive as an independent unit.

Other people also find themselves in situations in which they feel they have to have things well under control. Those recovering from alcoholism know that one drink will be the beginning of the end. Diabetics realize that straying from their diet could have serious consequences. Students on probation cannot afford to miss assignments if they want to stay in college. A mother who has an elderly parent in a convalescent home, small children to care for, and a husband whose work requires him to be out of town on business most of the week needs to organize her life situation, or her responsibilities will overwhelm her.

When we are in a situation that seems to require us to take charge, it may appear that our options are very few. Everything depends on us. Our families, our friends, and our society are counting on us to come through. The pressure can become great and the level of stress very high—especially if we seem to be slipping.

Why do people need to be "on top"? We have seen that the reasons are complex. Social learning and expectations, personality traits, and life situations all contribute to our wanting to be in charge of our circumstances. Of course, some people seem to need to have more control than others, but it would be fair to say that almost everyone is affected by the emphasis in our culture on being in charge of our lives.

WHAT ARE YOUR CONTROL NEEDS

How important is it for *you* to be in charge? Is your personality more the J type, liking a place for everything and for everything to be in its place? When things are changing around you, are you content to "go with the flow," or do you do your best to keep the change to a minimum?

In the Faith-Hardiness Inventory, you were asked to assess your need to be in control, to say how much you need to be on top of your situation. While some people have much stronger needs than others, most persons say that they have a need to be in control. Letting go is no easier for many of us than it was for George.

To get a little better idea of what your control needs are, ask yourself the following questions:

Do you like definite structure in your life? How hard is it for you to find things around your home? Is everything organized? It doesn't have to be neat to be organized. Some people have messy looking stacks of papers around, but they know what's in each stack! Does it bother you greatly if another member of the family takes something and puts it back in the wrong place?

Do you like to know in advance what you are going to do, where you are going to do it, and when? Could you be totally happy with a vacation that involved getting into a car, flipping a coin to see which road to take, and driving until you see something that attracts your interest enough to stop? Or would the lack of certainty greatly bother you?

When you are in a group, do you like to be a leader or a follower? While it might seem that only leaders have the need to be in charge, you may be one of those followers who likes to exercise a quieter control. How important is it to you to have a say in the direction a group takes? If a group decides to go in a different direction than you would like, do you attempt to redirect it? Do you refuse to go along and withdraw from the group? Either attempting to influence a group or pulling back from a group that is not heading where you would like it to go is a form of control, a way of taking charge.

Do others consider you a "take charge" person? Sometimes people who have a fairly high need for control really do not see themselves that way at all. Usually a member of the family or a close friend can help us see ourselves the way we come through to others.

There are many other questions that you might ask yourself to get some idea of how much you like to be in charge of what happens in your life. George probably never asked them. He just went about his life in the way that was natural for him until he came up against something that he could not handle in his usual way.

HOW FAITH-HARDINESS HELPS

There is nothing wrong with wanting to have some control over our life. There is nothing wrong with preferring an orderly, organized life-style to a more flexible and adaptable one. However, there are times in life when we are painfully reminded that we really do not have much control at all. And there are times when our best-laid plans go astray. What then do we do?

When the implications of his illness became clearer, George was faced with an important choice. One possibility would have been for him to deny the seriousness of his diagnosis. Perhaps the damage was not as severe as the doctor said. Maybe if he started taking care of himself, he would eventually be able to get back to his work. Or maybe he could just tough it out and overcome the heart attack by sheer force of will. In any case, if he chose to deny that things were as bad as they seemed, George would not really be able to accept and work within his limitations.

There are times when the faith-hardy approach to a problem is not to accept limitations just because someone says they're there. More than one person has walked again or talked again or even seen again after they were told that there was no hope. More than one inventor or explorer or researcher has refused to take seriously the word "impossible."

Yet there are times when the faith-hardy choice is to accept the reality that things have changed and life will never again be exactly the same. Those who have lost a loved one through death, those whose husband or wife has left and started another life with someone else, and those like George are examples of persons whose lives have been altered in a real way. Anything other than acceptance of the reality of that change will only block their mourning and recovery.

How does faith-hardiness help? Faith-hardiness helps in two ways: it helps us to hold on when faithfulness means never saying never. Faith-hardiness also helps us to let go when faithfulness calls us to "let go and let God."

HOLDING ON

The apostle Paul knew how to hold on in a faith-hardy way. When Paul was converted, the Christian community couldn't believe it. He never would have become God's messenger to the

Mediterranean world if he had accepted the verdict of those Christians who could see in him only a former persecutor. Paul never lost sight of the truth that with God all things are possible. He hung on to the vision he had experienced. Just as the scales had been removed from Paul's eyes, so his fellow believers eventually were able to see him as a man called by God to take charge of the gentile mission.

Martin Luther was counseled, even ordered, to let go of the gospel as he understood it and return to a safe and secure place within the church of his day. His refusal to take back the good news he was preaching was a faith-hardy act of holding on to the word despite incredible pressure to conform.

Pope John XXIII saw the opportunity for the church to be infused with a new spirit of love, and he held on to that hope as long as he lived. Mother Teresa, Martin Luther King Jr., Desmond Tutu, Simon Farisani, and many others less known to the world but dear to our hearts have shared their dreams in faith-hardy words and actions.

As confident Christians, faith-hardiness helps us hang on, because when we see difficult times with the eyes of faith, our eyes are open not only to the danger but also to the opportunity for those who trust in God. With Christ present and caring for him, the South African Simon

Farisani saw in his torture the opportunity to pray for his tormentors. With Christ present and caring for her, Mother Teresa saw past the terrible living conditions she had to endure to the challenge of working with God's homeless and helpless children. Even the world's acclamation could not keep her from returning to the special opportunity for service that only the eyes of faith can see.

More ordinary Christians like us have the promise of the same extraordinary, transformative power. "I will be with you always," Jesus said (Matthew 28:20). "Do not let your hearts be troubled and do not be afraid" (John 14:27). When we believe that Jesus stands with us in whatever situation we face, then we are able to see what only the eyes of faith can see. Stress is transformed to challenge when Christ is by our side.

Most of the time the challenge for a faith-hardy Christian is to hold on. When others around us give out or give up, the knowledge that Christ is with us can help us "keep on keeping on."

But it is not simply the holding on that is faith-hardy. The reason for a person's holding on can be because of fear, stubbornness, jealousy, or ignorance. For example, we saw how Kristin held on to an unsatisfying relationship with her husband, putting up with his demands and his absences until he finally decided to stay away for good. She may have believed that patiently enduring her unhappy home life was her only option as a Christian. She may also have feared doing anything else because she thought that her situation would worsen both for her and for her children. Perhaps she was unaware that holding on in this way rarely results in a change for the better. A faith-hardy way of taking charge in circumstances like this may require Kristin to take some risks. Despite her embarrassment, it probably would have helped had she talked with her pastor when the problems first started. Had she felt less alone, she might have risked confronting her husband long before he left. If Kristin and Todd had begun talking earlier, there may have been a different outcome.

What is faith-hardy is not our holding on to a destructive way of life, but our holding fast to the hope that Christ is close. When we find the courage to hold on in a situation because of our confidence that Christ is leading us toward health and wholeness, then we are both in charge and in Christ.

LETTING GO

But sometimes the only way to be in charge is to let go. As strange as that may sound, it is really only another way to say what we heard the apostle Paul say about being strong when he was weak. The strength Paul referred to was not his own. Rather, it was a faith-hardy awareness of how God works through our weaknesses in an empowering way. That's why Paul said that although he had many things he could boast about, instead he had chosen to "boast all the more gladly about my weaknesses, so that Christ's power may rest on me" (2 Corinthians 12:9).

George had always associated [control] with strength. His idea of taking charge was to be on top of the situation, overcome any obstacle, hang in until the end, and produce a product. After his heart attack he was no longer able to go about his life in the same way. In some ways George's circumstances remind us of what the apostle Paul was talking about just before he made his observations about strength and weakness. Paul mentioned that he had been given "a thorn" in his flesh (v. 8). It brought him down. Paul prayed not once but again and again that the problem would be taken away, but it wasn't. Instead, the answer of the Lord was, "My grace is sufficient for you, for my power is made perfect in weakness" (v. 9). It was then that Paul realized that when he was weak, then he was strong (v. 10).

George's thorn in the flesh took away one way of being in charge and offered another in its place. At first it was not at all easy for George to experience the strength that comes through weakness. When your identity is tied up in your work and you learn you can't do what you used to do, a part of you dies. Over the first few weeks George mourned his loss with angry words and uncharacteristic tears. He had once read the Bible all the way through, and now he found himself living the book of Job. But George had more than Job did. Job was silenced by a God he could not fully understand. George was reminded of the promise that the God revealed in Jesus Christ would be with him always.

As spouses and good friends often are, George's wife, Helen, was a sign that God's promise was not empty. She walked with her husband through the valley of the shadow, she accepted his anger and depression, and she helped him come out the other side by her faith that nothing could separate them from God's love.

The pastor helped, too. At first, when George was filled with questions about why this had happened to him, the pastor helped by not jumping in with easy answers. Instead, the minister encouraged George to find ways to express his thoughts and, more importantly, his feelings. "It's like the scaffolding has let go and everything has tumbled down on you," the pastor said.

"Yeah," said George with a sigh. "That's just how it feels."

Later, much later, there were other conversations, times when the pastor would ask questions.

"George, you've had to make a lot of changes in your life since the attack. Many of them have been hard and probably are not what you would have chosen for yourself had you remained healthy. Sometimes, though, people who become ill see some things that those of us who are rushing through life are more likely to miss. What are some things that you think I should keep in mind regardless of how busy I am?" In ways like this, the pastor helped George express what his illness had taught him about life and its meaning.

One of the most valuable insights George had was how easy it was for him to forget God and his family when things were going well. While he had always considered himself a good Christian and a good church member, George acknowledged to his pastor that he really didn't know what it was to be dependent on God. His health had always been good, his work had been admired, and he had never really faced a problem he couldn't handle. It took his illness to help him see how each day is a gift. George also saw that while work had consumed his time and his energy, the people who stood by him when he wasn't able to work were not those he worked with or those whose houses he had built. It was his wife and children who picked up the pieces with him and helped him go on. And it was his pastor and some of the members of the congregation who continued to call.

Then George got around to saying what was really on his mind. "All those years, Pastor, I thought I was somebody because of what I did. So I did it better than anybody else so I would be more of a somebody. The attack took that all away. Since then I've realized that I'm a somebody because I'm loved, and I don't have to do something special to be loved. I don't think I'd ever have learned that with the way things were before." Like so many of us, George was not easily able to let go of the idea that his self-worth was tied up in what he accomplished. His illness gave him his first real experience of what grace is all about. In his weakness he became strong. He took charge by letting go and putting his life in the care of Christ.

FAITH-HARDY SUGGESTIONS FOR TAKING CHARGE AND LETTING GO

Growth in faith-hardiness helps us recognize the times in our life when we need to let our confidence in the presence and care of Christ give us the courage to take charge of our situation and help move it toward reconciliation, healing, and wholeness. A faith-hardy perspective on life also frees us to let go in situations where we need to let God speak to us through our weakness. But whether holding on or letting go, what the faith-hardy seek first is to be "in Christ."

When is it faith-hardy to take charge? Kristin's life situation gives us a few clues:

When your marriage, your family, your job, or any other part of your life is not going the way you believe God wants it to go. The first step toward taking faith-hardy action is recognizing that God is involved in every part of your life. As long as you are only aware that *you* are unhappy with something, you are not likely to put it in a faith-hardy perspective. This is where the (w)holistic model can be of help. The model reminds us that anything that bothers us bodily or affects the way we think or feel or relate has at its heart a God-question. Faith-hardy persons look for that God-question. If you examine your relationships at home, at work, or in your congregation and realize that they are not what *God* wants them to be, then you have taken an important step toward faith-hardiness. Are there any parts of your life as a physical, mental, emotional, or relational person in which God might want you to hear his voice in a clearer way?

When you know God wants you to do something, if only you knew what it was. The second step toward being both in charge and in Christ is strengthening your conviction that God is not only involved in your life, but God also cares. Christ is not only present in the dark valleys of life; like a shepherd, he also leads us through them. That is his promise. The faith-hardy believe that promise. The crucial question is *how* the Lord will lead. The faith-hardy do not assume that they know God's will for them in every situation—so they ask. In the Faith-Hardiness Inventory the hardy Christian is more likely to pray and read the Bible. And the faith-hardy are more likely to get together with other Christians for mutual support. These are ways we can search out God's intention for us, asking what we need to let go of in order to take charge of our life in a faithful way. What are your ways of opening yourself to God's guidance and care? What would represent growth for you in this area?

When you believe that, with God, all things are possible. The faith-hardy Christian does not simply believe that all things are possible, but *with God* all things are possible. In order to take charge of our lives in a faith-hardy way, we may need to let go of the idea that we ought to be able to overcome our problems by ourselves without anyone else's help. The faith-hardy have a healthy sense of dependence on God and interdependence with other people. It is usually through other people that God chooses to work in order to accomplish his will in our lives. The turning point for Kristin was her pastor's visit and the courage that gave her to share her concerns with others. What was a very heavy burden for her to carry alone was made lighter both by her sharing and by the caring response of her family and friends. The knowledge that she was not alone gave Kristin confidence to make the choices that would lead her to a fuller life. Is there something in your life which, if shared with a pastor or another Christian, might take on new perspective and new possibility?

Sometimes the faith-hardy choice is more in the direction of "letting go and letting God." When is it faith-hardy to let go?

When taking charge could be a danger to yourself. In George's situation, the only way he could continue to go about his life in his usual, take-charge manner was at great risk to his physical health. The faith-hardy may choose to accept danger to themselves, as the apostle Paul did on his missionary journeys, or as a physician or nurse might do in order to treat someone with a contagious disease. But there is a difference between taking charge in order to serve God and taking charge in order to preserve our image of ourselves. If you were George, would you have been able to accept the limitations? How would your faith help you to let go?

When your self-image depends on your being strong. Perhaps those who most need to consider letting go are those who work so hard to be strong. George's illness gave him insight into how he had identified what he did with who he was. He never would have realized that he could be loved for himself if he had refused to let go of his usual way of living his life. I do not believe that God causes bad things to happen to us, but I do believe that God may have a very important message for us in times of illness or adversity. Since being in Christ is even more important than whether we take charge or let go, when difficult times come, the faith-hardy ask for God's guidance before they decide what to do. The faith-hardy also realize that, in some situations, the only way to be both in charge and in Christ is first to let go. When has your letting go helped you to deal with a situation in a way that increased your reliance on Christ?

When you believe that God will love you more if you take charge. Taking charge is the American way. It is our culture's answer to problems, and the message clearly comes through our parents and teachers. It should not be surprising that the same message can be heard in our churches. Yet from a theological point of view our acceptability to God is not because we take charge but because we are in Christ. When you think that God will love you more if you take charge, then it might be especially important for you to learn to let go. If you do not, then faith becomes a kind of works righteousness—trying to gain God's love because of what you do. That's exactly what George felt for most of his life. It took his illness to help him realize what grace means. Grace means we are free from the need either to take charge or to let go, because neither taking charge nor letting go makes us more acceptable to God. For Jesus' sake, God loves us as we are. Because God's love is assured either way, the faith-hardy are free to take the time to listen for the Lord's leading.

Think about a challenge that faces you at this time in your life. How is the Lord leading you? Is Christ encouraging you to take charge of that situation, or is he strengthening you so you can let go? Whether in the holding on or the letting go, how can you best witness to others that what really gives you confidence is that you are in Christ?

4

LEARNING HOW TO LOSE WITH GRACE

I was always told I should be a good loser. But I noticed that those who told me to be a good loser did not themselves like losing. It is hard to lose. It seems even harder to lose with grace.

Joe and Elaine, Kristin and Todd, George and Helen all faced loss situations. Some of their losses were obvious, others less so. Let's look at how each of these persons helps us to understand why dealing with loss is so difficult.

When Joe was told that he would have to accept a transfer or be let go, Joe immediately thought about his son, Bobby. Bobby was just ready to start his senior year in high school. A transfer at that time would almost have been a replay of the problem they were just getting beyond. Only two years earlier, when they lived in their previous community, Bobby had been cocaptain of the junior varsity team. He had hopes of making at least the second-string varsity as a sophomore. When Joe took the promotion, nothing he or Elaine said could persuade Bobby that the move would be good for their son.

Once the move had been made, Bobby was not the same. He did not even try out for the team at the new school. His grades dropped, and he began spending more time away from home in the evenings. Their problem with Bobby was what led Joe and Elaine to ask their new pastor for help. It took the better part of a year before Bobby was back to his old self. Elaine and Joe, especially Joe, had learned a lot in the process. The present transfer was different from the promotion because taking it was not of his own choosing. Still, Joe dreaded what it might do to the stability of his family.

Kristin was also concerned for her family, but in a very different way. Christy was eight and Melissa only four. Even though Todd had not spent as much time around the house the last year, still the girls were very attached to him. When Todd finally left, Kristin didn't know how to tell her daughters that Daddy wouldn't be living there anymore.

While we might be more conscious of the loss of Kristin and her daughters, Todd's leaving his family was also a loss for him. In fact, Todd's inability to reconcile himself to losses he had experienced in the past played a part in his decision to leave.

Todd himself had come from a broken home—a home broken not by divorce but by open conflict and constant bickering. His father drank heavily. When he was drunk he was mean. Too many times Todd had witnessed his mother taking abuse while he could only helplessly stand by. As he grew older, Todd wondered why his mother stayed in the marriage. She never did anything for herself and never got much pleasure out of anything. Todd promised himself that he would never let himself be so unhappy in a relationship. His mother paid little attention to him except to lay down the law. She was very strict and had high expectations of Todd, probably because she was afraid that he would grow up to be like his father. His mother's control was one of the few indications he was loved, so Todd quite understandably connected control with care.

Todd met Kristin when they were ninth-graders. He was lonely. She was too. And quiet. Kristin was so different from either one of his parents that Todd was certain he could be happy with her. When Kristin became pregnant, she and Todd married. They were just eighteen.

George and Helen married when they were 18, too. But it was a different generation. George never finished school. He enjoyed reading, but only in classes like history where he could read about real people who did real things. In most of the other subjects he became bored and restless.

Helen never regretted marrying George. He was a hard worker, and he worked long hours, especially after he started his construction company. But he was a good man, loyal to his family and devoted to it and to the church. It hurt Helen to see George unable to do the work that he loved so much. For a while after the heart attack, George was very depressed. When he was working, no matter how late he got home, Helen and her husband always had a quiet talk time. They brought each other up on the events of the day. It kept their intimacy alive and growing. Both of them enjoyed showing their love physically, and many evenings they went to sleep in each other's arms.

George's illness meant he was home all the time for a while, but he was much more withdrawn. Talking seemed to take so much energy, and Helen kept to herself anything that might upset her husband. As the open and honest sharing decreased, so did their feeling of intimacy. For several months George felt so low that the thought of sex didn't even cross his mind. As his depression lifted, George's interest increased, but so did his fear. He felt certain that he could not survive another attack. The vigorous physical relationship that Helen had enjoyed with her husband seemed gone forever. Helen had never had so much of her husband, nor so little. For the first time in her life she felt really alone.

WHY PEOPLE HAVE
A HARD TIME LOSING

If we take a closer look at major changes in the lives of people, we often find that, as in Helen's situation, a loss in the life of one member of a family often touches other members of the family as well—less apparently perhaps but often as painfully. Some psychologists and psychiatrists believe that behind most mental and emotional disorders lies some past, unresolved loss. Persons with a deprived childhood, children from homes in which there has been a divorce, victims of illness and accidents, those who love and lose someone important to them, survivors of genocide and wars all have to learn to handle loss.

Some people have a much harder time in loss situations than others. How loss is handled may be affected by our personality and by our past experiences with loss. Usually, though, when a major change is hard to accept, it is because the loss in some way threatens us at the deepest levels of our being.

HOW PERSONALITY RELATES TO LOSS

When we were talking about stress, we saw that some people are logical and analytical in the way they go about their lives. They may prefer to handle situations in a straightforward, matter-of-fact way, or they may be quite clever in thinking up solutions to problems. But whatever they do they try to do it without allowing their emotions to get in the way.

Other people, like Helen, are much more feeling-oriented. Helen was sensitive to her own feelings but even more aware of the feelings of others. People all the time send out verbal and nonverbal messages about how they are feeling. For example, a downhearted person may look down a lot and heave a sigh more often than most others. An anxious or impatient person may tap his finger or rapidly shift his gaze from object to object. There is, of course, no one meaning for any single gesture. Books that suggest a set interpretation for every move a person makes may be quite misleading. But the point is well taken that people send out signals of how they are feeling.

Somehow or other, a feeling person tends to pick up these clues faster and more naturally than other people. Like a thermometer tests the air temperature, feeling persons test the emotional climate. When they sense that something is amiss, they try to make things right. Feeling persons like their relationships to go smoothly, and they will try to keep them smooth no matter what it takes. When Helen saw George so depressed after his attack, she did everything she could to help him feel good again. This included keeping silent about her own needs, because she thought that saying anything about her needs would have made George feel worse.

Feeling people also have a special way of looking at time. When it comes to past, present, or future, a feeling type of person is much more likely to value the past. One sign of this is sentimentality. Feeling persons remember days gone by. They treasure those memories in their heart. Something someone says or does, a picture or a memento can bring a tear to the eye and a lump to the throat.

While this kind of holding on to the past can make a feeling person more of a romantic, it also means that feeling types are more vulnerable to loss. Loss means that whatever was is now gone. A person who by nature holds on to what once was finds it especially hard to face the fact that it is now gone for good. Consequently, a feeling type of person is more likely than others to deny that things have really changed. They keep hoping that somehow what has been lost will come back. This looking back over the shoulder can keep a feeling person from dealing with things as they are.

HOW THE PAST AFFECTS PRESENT LOSSES

While Helen has given us some idea of the part personality plays, there are other reasons why some people find it hard to lose. Joe, Elaine, and especially their son, Bobby, are examples of how losses in the past affect the way people handle losses in the present.

When his father changed jobs two years earlier, Bobby was devastated. Young people of Bobby's age are working through their identity. As with many teenage boys, Bobby's identity was tied up in his athletic ability. For a sophomore to have a place on a varsity team meant much more than just playing sports. It meant having a recognized place in the social structure of the school. Bobby probably would not have realized all this. He would have been more immediately conscious of having to leave behind both something he liked to do and the friends with whom he liked to do it.

When someone like Bobby has experienced a very significant loss in the past, the pain can remain so real that the possibility of another loss in the present can seem more than one can endure. Past losses are most likely to affect present feelings about loss if they have not been "worked through." This working-through process is called mourning.

Mourning can be successful or unsuccessful. Successful mourning does not mean liking a loss, but coming to accept it. Unsuccessful mourning is when a person denies a loss or minimizes it or simply resigns oneself to it. What makes such mourning unsuccessful is that the loss is never really dealt with in such a way that the person is free to go on with life.

We can deny loss without knowing what we are doing. Two years ago, when Joe came home and told his family about his promotion, he only presented the positive aspects of the move. That is a form of denial that many of us use from time to time. Another form of denial was Bobby's reaction. He simply refused to hear even the possibility of a move and went about his activities as if nothing had ever been said. It was as if by not thinking about it or not talking about it the undesirable event would go away. Elaine knew there was a loss involved, but she minimized it by pointing out the advantages of the move for Bobby. Denial in any of its forms, including minimization, does not help people deal with loss. When it came time to move, Bobby helplessly resigned himself to what was happening.

When people finally resign themselves to a loss, they have not really worked through their anger or depression. That's why when Bobby moved it was not the end of the story. He felt he had no choice except to follow his family, but his resentment came out in diminished performance at school and staying away from home at night. After the pastor became involved and there was a good airing of Bobby's grievances, things eased up a little. Bobby's energies were channeled into more constructive directions. But Joe and Elaine knew that Bobby was nowhere near ready to hear about another move because he really had never completely gotten over the last one.

THE DEEPER MEANINGS OF LOSS

A third reason why a loss may be so hard to handle is that a loss can have very deep meanings. Kristin and Todd's relationship gives us an example of how complex a loss situation can be.

Todd brought to his marriage with Kristin a history of unresolved losses. Only during his dad's infrequent periods of sobriety did Todd know what it was like to have a father. His home was organized around his alcoholic parent, which also meant the loss of a normal home. Because Todd's mother was overwhelmed by her situation, she was not really available to him. As in many alcoholic homes, Todd was expected to be exceptionally responsible, as if to make up for what his father didn't do. Todd never did much playing as a child, and at times he felt he had grown up and missed what it was like to be young. Todd carried all this unfinished business into his relationship with Kristin. What attracted him to Kristin was not so much the way she was as the way she wasn't. She wasn't anything like his parents!

Todd had not only lost his childhood, he had also lost the opportunity to see how to be a good parent. Children rely on their mothers and fathers to model effective parenting. When Kristin became pregnant, Todd was in no way prepared for his new role. Freshly out of high school, a new husband, a new father—the demands were greater than he could handle. Todd found escape with his cars. Under the hood or behind the wheel, Todd felt he had some control.

Because of his experiences early in life, especially his feeling of rejection by his parents, Todd always wondered if there was something wrong with him. Perhaps if he had been a better boy, his father might not have drank and his mother would have been happier. Just as in some way he felt that he had failed as a son, a part of him always expected to fail at whatever he did in life. When people have a serious question about their self-worth, their fears are sometimes realized. It's like a self-fulfilling prophecy: "Something's wrong with me, so things will turn out wrong."

People who are down on themselves often become critical of others. Eventually Todd came to blame Kristin for how unsatisfied he was. She didn't share his interests and wouldn't go with him to car shows. And she didn't care enough to set any limits on how much time he spent away from home. At least his mother had done that! But deep inside, Todd believed that he had failed in the relationship because he was a failure as a man. And failures fail. The other woman really meant nothing to Todd. She was just a way out.

Even though he was young, Todd felt very old. Life was passing by, and he somehow hadn't quite caught on to what it was all about. What finally got to him was seeing a wreck at a car rally. A driver he had admired, around his own age, crashed on a turn and was killed. That death caused Todd to think about himself. He wasn't sure why, but he knew he wasn't happy. Even though he loved his girls and would miss them, he didn't think he was a good father. He thought they probably would be better off with someone else—and probably Kristin would be too. He figured the best thing would be just to disappear—a clean break.

Some people have a hard time with loss because of their personality. Others have difficulty because of unresolved losses in the past. Often, though, our ability to handle loss is related to the deeper meanings of loss—how we really think about ourselves and life. And, at the deepest level, a loss always reminds us that life is not going to go on forever. Time is passing. Things come and go, are born and die. We, too, are dying. Time is slipping away. Todd felt that. Even more, George and Helen felt the closing in of time. Because they faced a serious health crisis, George and his wife were more conscious of the way that loss is linked with our mortality. But this deeper meaning is present in all forms of loss, even when we are not fully conscious of it.

WHAT IS YOUR WAY OF LOSING?

In the Faith-Hardiness Inventory, you were asked to answer several questions that have to do with loss situations. One of those questions was very direct. In a loss situation or a time of major change such as serious illness, accident, job loss, retirement, separation, divorce, etc., are you confident that the future will be better? Or are you more conscious of what has been lost or changed?

To help you look at your way of losing, you might give some thought to the questions that follow below.

Are you very sensitive to changes, especially those that upset your usual way of going about your life? While everybody is affected by losses, some people have more difficulty than others. George's story gave us an opportunity to discuss the J-type personality. The J person values being in control and having life orderly and organized. Of course, change and loss situations usually affect our feeling of how much we are in control. If you are a J person, does your desire to maintain control keep you from accepting a change or loss without a great struggle?

Are you, like Helen, a feeling person? If so, do your memories of "the way things were" ever get in the way of your being enthusiastic about the way things are? How much do you focus on the new possibilities a changed situation brings? Does it seem like the new could not possibly be as satisfying as the old?

What kinds of losses are most difficult for you to handle? Those who are oriented more outwardly toward the world of things and other people may be highly conscious of the loss of external things and social relationships. Those oriented more inwardly may have a particularly difficult time with the loss of the opportunity for private and personal time or the loss of an especially close interpersonal relationship with someone who truly understands. In other words, the kinds of losses or changes people find most difficult may vary from individual to individual, depending on what is important to that person.

How does your personality affect the way you express your feelings of loss? People differ not only in what is important to them, but also in how they actually deal with loss. Those who are more logical and analytical may try to "think" their way through a changing situation, in contrast to those who are more aware of their feelings. Those more outwardly oriented are likely to express their feelings openly, while those more inwardly oriented may keep their feelings locked inside. There are also differences in what is considered "normal" by the subculture in which we grew up. Some nationalities and subcultures are more expressive, others more reserved. The distress of one person or one group may be no greater than the other, but different ways of handling the stress of change and loss can present some very different pictures. How do you handle losing? What are you aware of inside, and what are others aware of as they see you from the outside?

We have seen that all losses are not the same, and what one person considers a loss may not be so much of a loss to another person. Furthermore, how people handle losses differs from culture to culture and individual to individual. But there is one thing all people have in common: change and loss, however understood, are unavoidable in life. What we now want to consider is if there is something about faith-hardiness that helps Christians face loss situations any differently than anyone else.

HOW FAITH-HARDINESS HELPS

Faith-hardy or not, a Christian has to learn to cope with loss because loss is a part of life. I believe a faith-hardy perspective helps Christians not by eliminating loss but by giving us a new way of looking at loss. In particular, faith-hardiness affects how we look at the past and the future.

FAITH-HARDINESS AND THE PAST

Not only feeling types of persons, but all of us Christians are people of the past. "Do this in remembrance of me," Jesus said at the Last Supper

(Luke 22:19). Christians remember. We even speak of each Sunday as a little Easter, a remembrance of our Lord's resurrection.

The Bible, which undergirds our faith and supports our ministry, records the history of God's mighty acts. In Christian education and preaching we are again and again drawn back to reflect on how God spoke through the men, women, and children of old. The more liturgical churches even construct their worship services in such a way as to replay the history of God's relationship with his people.

Therefore, when we Christians have losses to deal with, we can grow in faith-hardiness if we remember not to deal with them by ourselves, as if such a loss were happening for the first time. To the extent that we identify with those Christians who have gone before us, we have their experience and their witness to help us. That is why passages such as the Shepherd Psalm (Psalm 23) speak so clearly to us when we are going through dark valleys in our own lives.

The key to the comfort the people of God have found in facing losses through the ages is in our faith that we are not alone. That's what sustained the psalmist: "Even though I walk through the valley of the shadow of death, I will fear no evil, for you are with me" (Psalms 23:4). And that's what Jesus promised: "And surely I will be with you always, to the very end of the age" (Matthew 28:20).

The heart of faith-hardiness is our choice to place our confidence in Christ—a Christ who is present and caring during the losses and changes and stresses of our life. Christ's presence means that, however out of control we feel, the situation is not ultimately out of control because our Lord is with us. We see time after time in Scripture how God was working even in the most unfortunate circumstances and that none who called on him were forsaken.

When our focus is not on our own personal control but on Christ, then loss takes on a different meaning. The accent is no longer on the issue of control, but on the gaining of a higher sense of security. When feeling type Christians include in their memories the remembrance of a Christ who said, "I will not leave you comfortless: I will come to you" (John 14:18, KJV), then however painful the loss of a relationship is, it does not stand for the loss of *all* relationships. There is one who stands by us no matter what.

It takes a lot of courage to deal with change and loss. Sometimes our courage fails us and we try to deny or minimize or otherwise make a loss more manageable. Those who want to have a more faith-hardy perspective will be encouraged by looking in Scripture for stories about God's faithfulness to his people. The faithful in the Bible were no strangers to loss, but even more they were a people of hope. In every loss they faced there was a deeper meaning or purpose that eventually became clear. The faith-hardy believe there is meaning in every change, even though we may not perceive God's purpose at the moment.

FAITH-HARDINESS AND THE FUTURE

While Christians are a people of the past, we are also a people pointed toward the future. *"Marana tha"* was the call of the early church, which in Aramaic means, "Lord, come!" "Come, Lord Jesus," continues to be the cry of the church. In saying this we are proclaiming our faith-hardy conviction that the future belongs to God.

What are the practical implications of the future belonging to God? It means that when we suffer a loss we can risk being more trusting, more open to the new, and more confident that things will work out.

A loss is usually very threatening, as we have seen. It shakes our security and makes us uncertain of what we can count on. The natural tendency of persons who feel threatened is either to fight or to run. When George had his heart attack, there was no one to fight. His way of running was to withdraw. George's action of pulling back cut him off from others, including Helen, who was a primary source of support.

To grow as a confident, faith-hardy Christian is to allow ourselves to trust, even in the most difficult times, that our basic security is unshaken. While we may not be able to count on our health, our job, or even on some people, we can count on God. When we rely on that kind of security, then the energy we could use fighting or running can be used more constructively in looking for ways we can make the most of our changed situation.

Every new circumstance has its unknown perils. It also has its unknown possibilities. A faith-hardy perspective on the future looks for those opportunities. To be faith-hardy is to believe that God meets us at every turning point in our lives. God doesn't just catch up with us then, God *meets* us there. God is there before we are! To be open to the new, then, is only another way of saying that we choose to be open to God.

While we may not like every change that we face in life, when we believe that God is with us in the midst of that transition we have confidence that things will work out. After all, the apostle Paul has reminded us that nothing can separate us from the love of God in Christ Jesus. Nothing. Neither George's heart attack nor Kristin's divorce nor Joe's transfer. Such an attitude makes all the difference in the world because it places the loss in a context of caring. Our confidence is not in ourselves. We are all too often aware of our real limitations, and especially when nothing we do seems to make any difference. Our confidence is in God, who is at work in our situation to help us transform it into an opportunity for growth in Christ.

FAITH-HARDY SUGGESTIONS
FOR LOSING WITH GRACE

Since both the past and the future are in God's hands, faith-hardy persons are free to focus on the present. This is what lies behind Jesus' counsel to us: "Do not worry about tomorrow, for tomorrow will worry about itself. Each day has enough trouble of its own" (Matthew 6:34,).

If a particular day's trouble includes a loss situation, how can we face that loss in a more faith-hardy way? God's grace filled our yesterdays, and we believe it will fill our tomorrows. How can our trust in the grace of God help us in present times of loss? Here are some of the ways Christians can learn to lose with God's grace in mind.

Feel the present. First, faith-hardy individuals are free to feel the present moment. Included in the "nothing" that is able to separate us from the love of God is our feelings. Sometimes Christians think that they dare not feel certain feelings or they will not be acceptable to God. But Christians are saved by grace, not by their good feelings. When the faith-hardy suffer a loss, the feelings are as genuine and strong as they are for anyone else. Losing is painful, and grief includes not only sad feelings, but also feelings such as hurt and anger and anxiety. The faith-hardy are free to feel what they feel and to express what they feel, as did Job and Jeremiah, without fear that God will love them the less. Only by being in touch with our real feelings can we bring them before God for help and healing.

Growth in faith-hardiness means learning to grieve, but not as others do who have no hope (I Thessalonians 4:13). There is a difference between being in touch with feelings and allowing ourselves to be overcome by those feelings. The last word does not belong to our emotions but to God. Think of another time in your life when everything came tumbling in. Remember how you felt then—how it seemed like the problem would never end. How did God work in your life to pull you through? Did he speak to you through Scripture? Prayer? Preaching? Did God provide comfort and help through a church member? Did God work apart from the organized church through someone who may not even have believed in God but through whom you were able to feel God's presence and care? Our Christian hope is not only for tomorrow but for today. If this is a time of loss for you, how may God be working in your life right now to encourage and support you?

Live the present. Learning to lose with grace also means learning to forgive. When something goes wrong in our lives, it is natural to find something or someone to blame. The modern world of science seems to reject mystery and presents a cause-and-effect explanation for everything in the world. It is not that mystery is absent, as any physician can tell you who has seen an unexpected death or an amazing recovery for which there is no explanation. Much science is less scientific than it appears to be. But the modern myth continues to be that everything that happens is caused. Therefore, when something changes in our life, we look for whatever or whoever is at fault.

Looking for fault is looking back. It is not living the present. The only way to be fully in the present is to put behind us the blaming—of ourselves or of others. Forgiveness is God's way of giving us the present. Our forgiving of ourselves and each other is the best way for us to get beyond our losses and live more completely in the present moment.

Proclaim the present. The eyes of the psalmist were lifted up and the words came flowing out: "This is the day the Lord has made; let us rejoice and be glad in it. . . . Give thanks to the Lord, for he is good; his love endures forever" (Psalms 118:24, 29).

Those who want to grow in faith-hardiness will ask God to help them see each day in the context of his love and care. That is not always easy. Sometimes it was not easy for the psalmist, either. Walking through the valley of the shadow of death is not exactly the time when we would expect to hear that the Lord has made this day in which we should rejoice and be glad. But there was something that enabled the psalmist to proclaim the present, even when the going became very rough. It was summarized in four words: "You are with me" (Psalms 23:4). Faith in that promised presence is at the heart of the faith-hardy perspective on life, because with Christ, *presence* means compassionate care.

Proclaiming the present may take many forms: A prayer of thanksgiving; reaching out to someone else even when things are not going so well with us; getting up and going to worship services even though our heart is heavy and our body tired; sharing with a friend our confidence that, as stressful as our life is right now, we know that Christ will provide strength—these are some of the ways we proclaim the present. Another way is to practice what those who have struggled with a major loss or change in their lives often tell us is the only way they made it—live one day at a time. Again we recall Jesus' words: "Each day has enough trouble of its own."

Christians are at different points in their faith development. Some of us may need most to grow in feeling the present, others in living the present or proclaiming the present. The key to growth in the present is letting the Spirit open you to a faith-hardy perspective on the past and future. Knowing that Christ has enfolded the past in his love and guards the future against any lasting harm, confident Christians dare fully live each day, one day at a time, and trust our gracious God to take care of tomorrow.

5

How to Fight
a Good Fight

The apostle Paul told Timothy that we are to
fight the good fight of faith. Paul meant
that we are to let our hope in a living God be
reflected in our lives. Faith-hardy Christians
know that one important area where our commitment to Christ very much needs to be seen is
in the way we handle conflict. Tension between
people and among groups seems to be inevitable
in this world, even for Christians. But how we
choose to handle conflict can set us apart. It is a
powerful witness to be able to fight well and
faithfully.

Unfortunately, Christians are often no more
effective in conflict situations than anyone
else—and sometimes even less so. Long before
Kristin recognized that her marriage was in
trouble, she was conscious of feeling uneasy.
Being young and having a baby before there was
really time to get the marriage off the ground

was hard. Todd had to work two jobs for a while to pay the medical expenses, since they had no insurance. Day after day Kristin had the full care of Christy without any relief at all. That was especially draining until Christy was able to sleep through the night. Sometimes Kristin felt like she was sleepwalking through the days. Then Todd would come home and expect to be taken care of. He never changed a diaper or did a wash. Kristin smoldered but was silent.

Kristin was raised in a Christian home where children were to be "seen but not heard." Her parents did not like to raise their own voices, either, in front of the children. In fact, Kristin had never seen her mother and father fight. When she grew up she realized they must have had disagreements sometimes, but she had no idea how they were settled. Once, when she was about five, Kristin was playing in the living room and broke a figurine that was her mother's treasure. Kristin hid under her bed for the rest of the afternoon, afraid to come out. Her father came looking for her when she didn't respond to her mother's calls. She dreaded going out to the kitchen, but when she finally did, her mother just looked at her. Her mother didn't say a word. Kristin always remembered that incident. When she had angry feelings arise in her she thought there would be something wrong in expressing them. If people love each other, Kristin thought, surely they should know what they're doing wrong without being told.

WHY WE FIGHT THE WAY WE DO

Kristin's story gives us some ideas about why people handle conflict the way they do. Like Kristin, we all learn to fight one way or another. Most frequently we learn from our parents how conflict should be handled, even though they may never have discussed it with us. The most effective parental teaching is not what parents say but what they actually do. Kristin was taught that we should handle conflict quietly and privately, if at all.

LEARNING TO FIGHT

There are three forms of fighting that people are most likely to learn. One style is called passive; a second style is called aggressive; a third style is called passive-aggressive. Each of these leads to a distinctive and potentially destructive form of fighting.

Kristin's early training was in passivity. A passive person is restrained, uncomfortable around conflict, and usually glad to avoid it. If emotions are aroused, they are rarely expressed. What keeps a passive person from letting feelings out may differ from individual to individual. Passive men or women may not really know why they don't stand up for themselves in a more direct way. If we asked Kristin, she would have linked it with love. "Someone who loves you should know how you feel without your needing to tell them." One implication of this kind of thinking was that for Kristin to have to tell her husband her feelings would mean that he didn't love her enough to know them already. Many husbands and wives have the notion that such mind reading is a part of love. The lack of clear communication along with a passive approach to conflict made it unlikely that anything in Kristin's marriage would change. And nothing did.

The second form of fighting is more readily recognizable. Aggressiveness makes itself known because it tends to be noisy, invasive, insensitive, destructive, and sometimes violent. It is also natural. Under conditions of stress, the two most common animal and human reactions are to run away or to attack. Retreating is passive behavior. Attacking is aggressive.

When Joe was told about his transfer, he had an inner feeling of anxiety about the effect on his family, and he also had anger at his boss. Had he proceeded immediately to telling off his boss, putting his employer down for treating him so poorly and pointing out other injustices that had been done to himself and others over the years, that would have been an aggressive reaction. However natural such a reaction might be, it is not usually effective. Since aggression is an attack, it is understandable that most people respond to aggression with a counterattack.

Another form of fighting is called passive-aggressive. The putting of the two words together produces something that looks like the one and feels like the other. When Joe came home and told Bobby about the transfer, we saw that Bobby denied it as long as he could before finally resigning himself to the inevitability of the move. That has a passive feel to it, but later the aggression came out in indirect ways. Bobby began letting his schoolwork go and staying away from home. When Elaine would ask him to do something, he would agree but never get it done. His anger was coming out in roundabout ways. His parents felt something coming through Bobby's behavior without fully realizing what it was. Bobby himself may not have known that his passive and procrastinating behavior was a kind of aggression against his parents.

Neither passive, aggressive, nor passive-aggressive behavior is a way for Christians to fight faithfully. But Christians, along with most other people, are most likely to have learned one of these ways to handle conflict. Our way of reacting to a threat in our environment is probably similar to the way important people such as our parents reacted, as they are our earliest and most influential teachers. This was true for Kristin. However, sometimes we deliberately reject our parents' way of dealing with conflict. Todd heard loud, noisy arguments when he was at home. He decided there and then that his marriage would not be like that. Sadly, his indirect way of dealing with his dissatisfaction with Kristin was no more effective than his parents' aggressiveness. Neither impulsively acting on our feelings nor running away from them is the best that Christians can do.

FIGHTING AND FEELINGS

Feelings have a lot to do with how we fight. Since a conflict situation is in some ways a threatening situation, a feeling of fear may lead a person to pull back. Fear usually underlies passivity. Kristin feared being unloved. The part of passive-aggressiveness that is passive also has to do with fear. Bobby felt powerless. He feared resisting his father directly. Since he also felt angry, his anger came through in a variety of ways. Anger is the fuel of aggression.

Christians may not handle conflict very well because we have some special problems when it comes to anger. Somehow or other the message has come through that anger is not a feeling Christians should have.

Helen felt the burden of her anger especially keenly. Unlike Kristin, Helen's understanding of what love means was linked not with mind reading but with good communication. Helen and George had always worked very hard to see that they had time to talk with each other. They did not assume that either would necessarily know what their partner was thinking or feeling unless they said it out loud. That's one of the reasons why George's withdrawal after his heart attack was so difficult for Helen. She understood why he would be depressed, but she didn't understand why he had pulled back from her. Helen was afraid to press George too hard for fear of causing him a setback, but the longer she put up with things as they were, the angrier she became.

When Christians have strong negative feelings but believe that they shouldn't have them, they may try to bury them. But what we have learned about passive-aggressiveness suggests that feelings don't just fade away. Feelings find a way to get expressed one way or another. Rather than through behavior, as with Bobby, suppressed anger may come out in the form of bodily symptoms. Intense anger that is held inside can make a person ill. Or a person might sit on anger that is held inside for a long time and suddenly have it explode in an impulsive, aggressive outburst. Generally there is real regret when something like that happens, both for what is said and the way it is said, but it is hard to "unspeak" words once spoken. Helen was especially concerned that something like that could happen if she didn't find a way to reach George.

WHAT IS YOUR WAY OF FIGHTING?

How do you handle interpersonal conflict? Do you fight a good fight? Here are some questions that may help you get a better idea.

What message do you bring from your past about feelings and fighting? Is it acceptable for you to have strong negative emotions, or do you believe such feelings are bad?

When you have a feeling of anger, are you more inclined to express that feeling in a passive or an aggressive way? Do you think that raising your voice in anger is wrong? Do you believe that "time will take care of it"? Does "turning the other cheek" mean that you should not speak up for yourself when you think you have been wronged? When you are convinced you are in the right, do you believe that you should argue your position strongly regardless of whose feelings might get hurt?

Were you able to identify more with Kristin's way of handling anger or with Bobby's and Todd's? Or with Helen's? If your employer were to have come to you with the word that Joe received, how would you have handled it? Does the time, place, or circumstance affect how you express your feelings? Are you aggressive in some situations but passive in others? What accounts for the difference?

The last time there was a conflict in your congregation, what did you do? Did you stay out of it entirely or at least avoid it as much as possible? Were you aggressively vocal about your opinion and feelings? If the outcome of the conflict was a decision that you did not like, did you passive-aggressively stay away from services or withhold your offerings?

In your community, how comfortable are you with political issues? Politics have to do with power, and there is always conflict when it comes to the handling of power. People who feel powerless, as Bobby did with his parents, may become passive. Not only individual Christians but whole congregations may feel powerless in the life of a community and therefore be passive participants in decisions that affect the quality of life of everyone. What is your personal approach to community power struggles? Is it similar or different from the approach your congregation takes?

Since passive, aggressive, and passive-aggressive ways of handling conflict are neither that effective nor faithful, do you see any alternative for Christians? Effectiveness can be judged by the

way people feel about the outcome of the conflict. What might be the marks of faithfulness
that you would look for?

HOW FAITH-HARDINESS HELPS

The Faith-Hardiness Inventory asked you to say
whether you are more likely to see a situation of
interpersonal conflict as potentially destructive
or as a possible way to make things better.
Remember that how we took at a situation
makes all the difference in what we do about it.
Growth in faith-hardiness is related to our
increasing ability to see things from the perspective that Christ is present and caring in the midst
of our concerns.

It was a faith-hardy step that took Helen to
see her pastor. She didn't mention her anger at
first. She talked about how hard it had been for
George and how well he was handling his recu-
peration. But eventually her irritation and impa-
tience began to come through, and the pastor
picked up on the clues. "I'm amazed, Helen, that
you're doing so well," her pastor said. "I
remember a time when I had a great many
demands on me. It seemed like give, give, give
and no place to turn to get my own needs met. I
felt frustrated and even angry. Have you ever felt
like that?" Simply hearing such words from her
pastor's lips in a nonjudgmental way gave Helen

all the permission she needed to share the feelings that made her feel most guilty.

In the discussion that day and the counseling sessions that followed, Helen learned that feelings themselves are not good or bad. What counts is what we do with those feelings. Passively sitting on them usually results in no improvement in our situation. Aggressively acting on them may harm others or ourselves in some way. Passive-aggressive communication is ineffective because it is indirect and does not build the trust that is necessary for resolving differences.

An alternative to the three most common forms of fighting is called *assertiveness*. Assertiveness is dealing with feelings by accepting them and expressing them appropriately and directly to the person we're in conflict with. However, not all people mean exactly the same thing when they use the word *assertive*. Some think that assertiveness can come through as aggressiveness unless the assertive person is *responsibly* assertive. Responsible assertiveness not only recognizes our own rights in conflict situations but also the rights of the other person or persons involved. From a Christian perspective, this kind of responsible communication is an important form of caring.

After checking with George's physician, the pastor counseled Helen to be as responsibly assertive as possible with George, because the breakdown in her communication with her husband was a greater risk than a confrontation. But before Helen felt comfortable in doing that, she had to come to accept her anger as a gift from God.

THE BIBLE AND ANGER

The Bible makes many references to anger. Some of them present anger in a pretty poor light. Since anger "resides in the lap of fools," according to Ecclesiastes, we should not be quick to anger (Ecclesiastes 7:9). A person with a short fuse is likely to handle things inappropriately (Proverbs 14:7). Angry persons stir up strife and are bad company to keep (Proverbs 22:24-25; 29:22).

But the New Testament puts anger in a perspective that is especially helpful. "In your anger do not sin," is the word we find in Ephesians 4:26. The New English Bible conveys the meaning of this verse even more clearly: "If you are angry, do not let anger lead you into sin." It is not being angry that is sinful, but rather what we do with that anger. We are encouraged not to "let the sun go down" while we are angry (v. 26). Letting the sun go down means holding onto our anger—not expressing it, but nursing it. Anger that is held onto turns into resentment. And conscious resentment eventually turns into unconscious hostility. A hostile person is quite unaware of how deeply angry—and how destructive—he or she really is.

Anger, therefore, can and often does lead to estrangement. It separates, pushes away, sets up barriers to communication, and makes fellowship impossible. That is why the Bible says that when we bring our gifts to the altar, if we remember that our brother or sister has something against us, we are to leave our gift before the altar. Our first and more important offering is to go and first be reconciled to that person (Matthew 5:23-24). How can the faith-hardy see anger as a gift of God? As a reminder of a broken relationship, our awareness of anger is meant to prompt us to do whatever we can to become reconciled.

Are there other ways in which anger represents a challenge and an opportunity to grow in faith-hardiness? I think anger is a gift that also helps us to clarify our values. This clarification enables us to take the steps that need to be taken toward healing and wholeness in our lives and the lives of others.

ANGER AND VALUES

When we discussed the (w)holistic model we saw that the physical, mental, emotional, and social dimensions of ourselves are interrelated. What affects us in one area affects all the rest. From a (w)holistic perspective, anger interacts with our body and our thinking and affects our relationships. That is why some people who keep intense anger inside develop physical symptoms and why others are hard to get close to. But the deeper truth of the (w)holistic model is that at the heart of every significant issue in life is a God-question. Anger is among the significant issues in the life of a Christian.

What is the God-question at the heart of anger? When anger is a reaction to threat, our anger says that something we value is being threatened. Therefore the working through of our anger in a conflict situation gives us an opportunity to clarify our values, including our ultimate values.

Working through our anger requires that we know a little more about the nature of anger. Anger is sometimes said not to be a primary emotion at all. That means that if you scratch the surface of anger, you find another feeling. When Joe was told about the job transfer, he was anxious and fearful about what the future held for him and his family—but he felt angry. When Bobby had to move, he was frustrated by what seemed to be a very unfair turn of events—but he felt angry. When Todd neglected Kristin and George pulled away from Helen, they both were disappointed, hurt, and sad—but they felt angry. Anger in the lives of these people pointed toward other feelings: anxiety, fear, frustration, disappointment, hurt, sadness.

When I am angry and that anger is getting in the way of my functioning or relating, I ask myself what the feeling is beneath my anger. If it is anxiety or fear, what is it that I am really afraid of? How can it injure me in a lasting way? If it is frustration, what is it that is frustrating me? Is there an interpersonal or vocational goal that is being blocked or threatened? What difference does that goal really make from the standpoint of the kingdom of God? If it is disappointment, hurt, or sadness, what is the real and most painful loss? Is it the loss of a dream or the loss of a relationship or the loss of a certain image of myself?

Questions like these help me to use my anger in two ways. First, my anger is not allowed to be an end in itself. It leads me to a fuller awareness of my underlying feelings. Second, my deeper feelings help me to become more conscious of my values. I have given so much importance to something that a threat to it makes me angry (anxious, fearful, frustrated, hurt, etc.). What is it that I value so much? Is it a true and lasting value, or is it a false value that five years from now will make no difference at all? Does what I value lead me toward or away from my commitment to Christ? Christ is by my side, present and caring. Does he share my value?

When Helen became aware that the anger about which she felt so guilty could be understood as a gift from God, she began to go to work on it in a faith-hardy way. Her anger was a sign of her estrangement from George and the need for reconciliation in the relationship that meant so much to her. In looking at what feelings lay beneath her anger at George she saw that she was not only hurt that George had pulled away, she was also afraid that it would always be like this. Would they ever again be close the way they once had been? Why had this happened to them? She and George had always tried to be good people, and they had hurt no one. Helen was able to admit for the first time that she felt God had let her down. Her pastor helped her to express her anger at God. By not defending God or pulling away from Helen, the pastor was a visible reminder that Christ stood with her even in her anger.

FIGHTING A GOOD FIGHT

With her feelings identified and expressed, Helen was ready to learn from them. Until she became frustrated in this way, Helen had not really known how emotionally dependent she had been on her husband. Had she been too dependent, to the point where there had been no room in her life for anything or anyone but George? His illness was a painful reminder that nothing in this world is permanent. Her dependency on George, as well as his on her, needed to be embraced by an even more fundamental awareness of their mutual dependency on God. The illness had shattered their security and strained their relationship. But it could help them to reestablish their relationship on even more solid ground.

What was required for Helen was the same thing that is required of each of us once we allow our feelings to help us understand ourselves and what is important to us. If we have a false or misplaced value, we need to come to terms with it and let it go. If our value is not misplaced, we need to fight for it. Helen was convinced that her relationship with George was worth fighting for.

Suppressing her feelings had not worked and really could not work for Helen. She needed to take responsibility for her own feelings and, without blaming George for how she felt, let him know what was in her heart. She needed to communicate clearly what she wanted and needed in her relationship with her husband. To respect George as a person, Helen needed to make certain that she was asking for his response rather than demanding it.

A faith-hardy assertiveness such as I am describing is based on a healthy appreciation for ourselves as children of God who have worth and value. What underlies passivity can be a sense that our thoughts and opinions and feelings are not really that important and have no right to be expressed. Underlying aggressiveness can be a belief that only our own thoughts and opinions and feelings are really important and deserve to be heard. The faith-hardy understand that our worth as persons is not of our own making but given by God. As God's child, gifted with thoughts and feelings, I have something to say and a responsibility to say it in a caring way. Those with whom I am in conflict, who are also children of God and who are gifted in their own ways, have a right to be heard as well. Reconciliation between us Christians (and between us and those outside the faith) is more likely to happen when we are aware of our mutual giftedness and responsibility toward one another.

As Helen grew in a faith-hardy perspective, she came to perceive the conflict she was in not simply as a threat, but as a possible way to make things better. The way was not without risk. The consultation with George's physician helped her feel more confident that she could express her feelings to her husband without danger to him. But there were other risks. George might not respond the way she wanted him to. He might deny that there was any problem at all or accuse Helen of being unsympathetic and lacking in understanding of all that he had been through. But he also might hear her, and together they might not only regain but go beyond what they had shared in the past. In her prayers

Helen asked God to open them both to that kind of future.

FAITH-HARDY SUGGESTIONS FOR GROWTH IN FIGHTING FAITHFULLY

To be saved by grace means that we do not need to resolve our conflicts in order for God to accept us. But because we are saved by grace, we are free to take a good look at those things and people that make us angry and to see how we can let our feelings lead us toward reconciliation. We are called to be reconciled to God and each other, and reconciliation is the reason for learning to fight a good fight. Here are some suggestions for learning to fight more faithfully.

Whether it is your own or someone else's anger that you are concerned about, ask yourself, what is the feeling underlying the anger? You will be able to deal with your own anger or respond (not react) to someone else's anger more effectively and faithfully if you understand what lies behind it. If Christians know that anger is a signal, a face—usually a false face—it can help us not react with anger. How good are you at "reading" anger in this way? Practice with yourself. The next time you feel angry, stop and ask yourself what feeling your anger is carrying along with it.

Whatever the deeper feeling that underlies strong anger, it needs to be expressed. Helen may not have felt able to express her feelings to George, but she needed to share her anger with someone. If she didn't, she would remain angry and the sun would have continued to go down on that anger many more times. Eventually her resentment would have made reconciliation even more difficult. Sharing in an appropriate place the feelings that underlie our anger is faithful because it is the first step toward restoring a broken relationship. You might select someone who knows you well (but not someone you are currently angry with) and discuss how you typically deal with conflict and anger.

Use conflict situations to help you clarify your values, as Helen did. Practice seeing beyond your feelings in this way. Let anger be a gift from God, disclosing false or misplaced values and pointing you to a fuller life. Consider how congregational conflict can be a possible way to make things better, and how community conflict can lead the way toward greater justice for all citizens. If our anger reflects our perception that people are being treated in an unfair and inhumane way, then we need to share our concern with the Christian community. One person can challenge the oppressive structures of society, but that challenge is much more likely to lead to change if it is made by all Christians. This prophetic dimension of our faith is as vital in our time and place as it was in Israel.

How much do you know about assertiveness? Assertiveness may not come as naturally to you as aggression or passivity. Christians who learn to be assertive will be less likely to attack others when they are angry. They will also be less inclined to keep their feelings inside where they can turn into resentment. Community agencies like the YMCA and YWCA, mental health centers, and college continuing education programs offer programs in assertiveness training. While one doesn't have to be a Christian to be assertive, we are helped to fulfill our ministry of reconciliation by learning to use such an approach in our relationships.

Because anger is the face displayed by many of our different feelings and may mean different things at different times, the Bible and Christian theology rightly identify it as a very important emotion. Rather than praying that we overcome our anger, we need to pray that we will understand it and let it lead us to a fuller understanding of ourselves, our situation, and our life's direction. The faith-hardy perspective that Christ is with us in the midst of our conflicts can help us to see the challenge that conflict represents. Christ also helps us to recognize that some ways of fighting are more faithful than others. Facing our feelings head-on, while respecting the rights of others no less than our own, is a faith-hardy choice that increases the chance of reconciliation. And for the confident Christian, that's what fighting faithfully is all about.

6

WEARING THE
WHOLE ARMOR OF GOD
(WITHOUT CLANGING)

To be a person involves our bodies, minds, feelings, relationships, and ultimate values. In the Faith-Hardiness Inventory, you ranked the physical, mental, emotional, social, and spiritual dimensions in the order of their importance to you. While most Christians rank the spiritual as either first or second in importance, I pointed out that the spiritual does not really belong on such a list as if it were only a part of life. A better way to represent the relationship between the spiritual and the other dimensions of life is with the (w)holistic model. Through the use of the center "L," the model visually shows that the spiritual is at the heart of every physical, mental, emotional, and social concern.

In this book, I have identified a potential problem in each of these areas of life and revealed the spiritual center of that concern. "Putting Stress in Its Place" enabled us to show how faith-hardiness helps confident Christians deal with stress as something that affects the body but is much more than a physical problem. In the chapters "How to Be in Charge and in Christ," "Learning How to Lose with Grace," and "How to Fight a Good Fight," we lifted up the spiritual issues at the heart of the difficulties we Christians have with control, loss, and conflict.

Now we turn to another area where having a faith-hardy perspective helps in our approach to our spiritual life. We'll see that the faith-hardy express their spirituality in many different ways. But we'll also find that there are some commonalities among Christians that those who would like to grow in faith-hardiness may want to keep in mind.

Let's begin looking at spirituality by contrasting the approach to faith taken by Elaine and George. Elaine was raised in a Christian home where faith ran deep and was a constant source of strength. We see illustrations of this reliance on God in the way Elaine's father handled his terminal illness and, later, the way her mother dealt with her bereavement. In her time of crisis there was no question in Elaine's mind about where to turn. The church, her pastor, and Christian friends all played a very important part in

Elaine's life. She believed that God not only promised help to those in distress, God also provided it. The form in which Elaine experienced that help was primarily through her fellow believers.

While Elaine was more likely to set aside time to pray, George was inclined to make work his prayer. Like his father before him, George offered up to God his integrity as a workman and his commitment to doing his best for others. While he attended church services with some regularity, especially after he married Helen, and had once even read the Bible all the way through, George was not overly involved with the church. He appreciated the structures of the church and the way it helped people to organize their lives. He liked the emphasis on ethics and morality. But he did not see the church as a primary resource in times of trouble, as his life had been largely trouble free until his heart attack.

WHY WE APPROACH
GOD DIFFERENTLY

Within the experience of Elaine and George we can find some of the reasons why we Christians develop so differently in our spiritual lives. Reflected in our spirituality is our heritage, our personal preferences, and our life circumstances.

A DELIGHTFUL INHERITANCE

The psalmist spoke of the delightful inheritance he had from the Lord (Psalms 16:6). He understood himself in relation to the giver of all good gifts. The psalmist's song of praise was a way of expressing thankfulness for what he had received from God.

Christians at different times and in different places have found a variety of ways to offer praise and thanksgiving, to make petition, to confess and seek absolution, to live in a way that expressed their faith. There is no one way to do these things. Those Christians who travel through America, Europe, or third world nations come back impressed with the tremendous variety of ways in which God is worshiped.

Elaine had the heritage of a liturgical church. From her earliest years on, Elaine's parents took her to services on festival occasions in the parish. She knew something about seasons of the church year, altar paraments, and ministerial vestments. She discovered that the church had a rhythm to it, just as the faith as she had come to understand it moved from birth to death and from death to resurrection. When her own life took on the rhythm of crisis, which also has the marks of dying and rising again, Elaine quite naturally saw the church as a primary source of strength.

George's training as a child was less formally religious. His father had emigrated from a country that had many ugly conflicts between members of different churches. George's father had become soured on the traditional church. He kept the ethical values but threw away the ecclesiastical framework. If it had not been for his mother, and then Helen, George probably never would have joined a church. What George learned as he grew up was that it was important to be a good person, fair in one's dealings with other people and someone whose word could be trusted. George's first exposure to the Bible was as a book that helped people to live the right way.

After they were grown up, neither George nor Elaine really gave much thought to just how much their personal and family backgrounds affected their approach to religion. George was religious in his way, and Elaine was religious in hers. Even though they eventually became members of the same congregation, their basic attitudes and feelings about the practice of their faith remained very much a reflection of their own individual history.

A MATTER OF PREFERENCE

Along with what we inherit from the past, the development of our spiritual lives is affected by our personality preferences. Elaine was a very outgoing person. When she was feeling a little low on energy, being around other people would usually charge her back up again. Her more social orientation was evident in her belonging to the women's group and her eagerness to talk with the members of her circle and the pastor when Joe came home with news of the job transfer. Elaine was particularly sensitive to stresses in her relationships with her family or friends, and she was willing to be very flexible if she felt that it would help others.

George was more inclined to keep things to himself. He rarely shared his more personal thoughts or feelings with anyone other than Helen. Even that stopped for a while after he became ill—until Helen confronted him. George was a man of principle and purpose. He knew what was fair, did what was fair, and expected others to do the same. He admired organization as one way to insure that things were done decently and in good order. George believed things were more likely to be seen as fair if everyone knew where they stood and what to expect.

When it came to spiritual discipline and religious practices, it should have been obvious that Elaine and George had very different priorities. Elaine was interested in the church having many small groups and opportunities for people to be with each other. She was one of those who wanted to have a time during the service for everyone to go around to others and greet them.

She liked preaching that told stories of people and the way that God was active in their lives. She liked prayer best when it was a spontaneous and shared experience of the whole congregation. She believed that the only way for prayer to be answered was for Christians to get up and do something about the situation and let God use them as part of that answer. Elaine thought that the most important ministry of the congregation was to call on members and prospective members. But that would not do much good unless the church was a warm and inviting place to come to. Elaine did all she could to make the congregation such a place.

Not only because of his different heritage, but also because of his personality preferences, the priorities George held for the church and in his own devotional life were quite different from those of Elaine. George was not as interested in the social function of the church. He didn't mind if others attended various groups, but he had little desire to do so himself. He did, however, like the service to be well-prepared, and he liked worship to start and end on time. He appreciated a quiet time for reflection and in general felt more comfortable when the service was more solemn and without surprises. In the pastor's sermons, George listened for guidance about how best to live a Christian life. He also wanted the sermons to deal with current events and to suggest ways to understand that which happens around us, especially in the local community. George saw Sunday worship as pretty much taking care of his spiritual needs for the week. Starting on Monday morning, the way for him to be religious was to do the best job that he could.

THE TIME IN OUR LIFE

Our heritage and individual personalities account for most of how we choose to approach God, but we are also influenced by the period of life we are in. As the mother of a school-age child, Elaine was very conscious of the example she was setting for Bobby. Bobby, like many teenagers, put a lot of things ahead of attending church. Two years earlier, when they had first moved, one of the ways Bobby protested the move was by boycotting church services. It was only after the pastor showed some special interest in him that Bobby started attending the youth group—clearly for the pastor and not for his parents, he wanted it understood. Elaine, knowing how important her parents' model had been for her as she grew up, was eager not to let her son down in any way. Of course her family history and personal preferences made providing such an example relatively easy for her.

Being older, with his children grown and living out of town, George's personal religious practices were less related to child-rearing and were more like his work ethic, a way to express the values that he had developed throughout his life.

After his attack and during the recovery period, George was a lot more dependent on others than he had ever been before. The change in his life circumstances helped him understand the importance of calling and making other kinds of personal contact with those who could not make it to church. Both the pastor and other members of the congregation continued to let him know that he was thought about, and their support not only of him but also of Helen meant a lot to him. Though George still did not see himself as someone who could ever lead the visitation committee, he came back to church after his attack with real appreciation for those who did.

While the influence of our heritage, our personal preferences, or our life circumstances may vary in strength from person to person, the spiritual life and discipline of all Christians is affected in some way by these three factors. Sometimes what we consider to be the "right" way is nothing other than the way we have learned, or the way we prefer, or the way that seems most important to us in the immediate situation. Knowing how our approach to God has been shaped in these ways can be freeing and lead us to a more fulfilling spiritual life.

WHAT IS YOUR "SPIRITUAL PATH"?

The idea of an individual approach to God or a personal spiritual path needs to be correctly understood. If we are not careful, our emphasis can be put in the wrong place.

The witness of the Bible is that the relationship between God and God's people does not start with us. God becomes our God not because we find the right way to come before the Lord, but because God chooses to draw near to us. God takes the initiative, calls us, gathers us, and enlightens us.

When we speak of an approach to God or a spiritual path, then, we need to be thinking not of the way we win God's favor, but the way we respond to the favor God has already shown. Our worship and our personal devotional life is our response to God's grace.

One way we respond is with thanksgiving and praise. Christians say "thank you" and praise God in many different ways. Elaine and George are examples of two possible paths. To learn more about your own, you might answer the following questions.

What is the heritage you bring to your spiritual response to God? How has your nationality, your culture, your family background, and your experience in a particular denomination or congregation affected what you consider to be the best or most appropriate way for you to worship? How does that heritage influence the kind of music you prefer and the flow of the service that is most appealing to you? How does it affect the degree to which you are comfortable with members speaking out during the service or actively participating during worship in other ways? One way to discover the effect of your background is to talk over your present preferences with someone who likes a very different style of worship. Then compare your background and life experiences to see what light that might shed on what pleases each of you today.

What connections can you make between your worship preferences and personal devotional practices and your gender, marital status, training or vocation, the presence or absence of children in your home, the stage in life you are going through, and any crisis that you have experienced? A way to see what difference your life circumstances make is to compare your spiritual path ten years ago and five years ago with your path today. If they are not the same, what accounts for the change?

Is your response to God more action-oriented or more reflective? Do you, like Elaine, appreciate a more outgoing, social form of worship and spiritual discipline, with emphasis on Christian fellowship and corporate activity? Or are you more similar to George, valuing a quiet, reserved, even private approach that draws on your inner resources? Are you quicker to do a good deed than to read the Bible or pray? Is your focus more on fellowship or on the sharing of Christian ideas and principles?

Does structure help you worship? In the expression of her spirituality, Elaine was more flexible and willing to adapt than was George. He looked for discipline and order. Do your personality differences lead you in the direction of a spirituality with plenty of room for spontaneity, or are you more inclined toward a particular structure or rule of faith that will help you be more disciplined?

What balance do you maintain between the ministry of the church and the mission of the church? Do you put your emphasis on the specific, the concrete— the budget, the building, and programs? Or when you think of the mission and purpose of the church, do you think in more general, universal terms?

While God has chosen to come to us in Christ Jesus, who is "the way and the truth and the life" (John 14:6), there is no one way to respond to our Lord except to love him with all of our heart, soul, mind, and strength (Mark 12:30). That love can be expressed in many forms. Jesus said that our discipleship is known in our love for each other (John 13:35), and the apostle Paul pointed out that the most eloquent words, if loveless, are like a noisy gong or a clanging cymbal (1 Corinthians 13:1). When we Christians clash about ways to worship and practice our devotion, it comes through to the world not as our desire to put on the whole armor of God, but only as so much clanging.

This is not to say that the forms of our spiritual expression have nothing to do with our faith in Christ. Our response to God is communication, and we all know that how we say something often communicates a stronger message than what we actually say. It is also true that some forms are not options; they are "givens." For example, as someone has observed, Jesus did not say, "*If* you pray," he said, "*When* you pray . . ." (Luke 11:2; italics added). But it is nevertheless important that we recognize just how many of our preferences in spiritual expression have been shaped by significant persons and events in our lives and how much our personality is involved in the choices we make. A hardy faith helps us keep such things in perspective so we are less likely to confuse *our* way with *the* way.

HOW FAITH-HARDINESS HELPS

Faith-hardy persons are able to keep any approach to spirituality in perspective by shifting the attention from what we do to what God has done for us in Jesus Christ. Our confidence as we face the challenges of life is not that we have done the right thing in the proper way, but that God has done the needed thing in a grace-full way. God has come to us, is for us, stands with us, stands under us (understands), and leads us. When we don't even know how to pray as we ought, "the Spirit . . . intercedes for us with groans that words cannot express" (Romans 8:26). The confidence of the faith-hardy is that we are not, never have been, and never will be alone. God in Christ Jesus is with us.

The faith-hardy focus on fellowship with Christ has three important implications for living a Spirit-led life. First, growth in faith-hardiness means letting the presence of Christ make more and more of a difference in what we see and say and do. Second, growth in faith-hardiness requires nurturance and support. Third, growth in faith-hardiness means understanding our fellowship with Christ in an ever expanding way.

THE DIFFERENCE CHRIST MAKES

Of all the questions in the Faith-Hardiness Inventory, the most critical is the final question: "In a difficult situation lasting more than a few days, how conscious are you of Christ's presence and care?" But the answer to that question is not found where you would expect to find it. You may have answered that for you Christ is a very real and caring presence in such a time, but the *real* answer to how aware you are of the Lord's presence is in the difference that awareness makes in what you see and say and do.

A helpful discipline is to go back over the Faith-Hardiness Inventory and answer each question again as you would *if you were really convinced that right now,* in the midst of whatever life situation you find yourself, *Christ is literally by your side.* How would Christ being close enough to touch affect your feeling of well-being, your perception of stress, your sense of control, your hopefulness in time of loss, your confidence in time of conflict? Really let yourself believe that the Lord is with you and see what difference Christ's presence can make in your confidence as a Christian!

Of course the point is that Christ *is* really present with us. It's just that we Christians, faith-hardy or not, sometimes forget it. Or Satan blinds our eyes to it. Or our misplaced confidence that we are sufficient in and of ourselves to meet the challenges of life makes Christ pale behind our pride.

But despite what stands in the way of our perceiving it, the promise of presence has been given and God keeps his promises. Growth in faith-hardiness is a peeling away of the scales from our

eyes so that we can see with ever-increasing clar-
ity and confidence the promised Christ!

How are those scales removed from our eyes?
I do not believe we can do it by ourselves. A
faith-hardy perspective on life is not an accom-
plishment, it is a gift. But most importantly, it is
a gift God intends for us all. How do we know
that? The Bible is very clear that Jesus died for
all and rose again for us all. To all who come to
know him, Christ's continuing presence is
promised. And Jesus gave us the Great Commission to go into all the world baptizing and
teaching, so that everyone will have the chance
to know him.

But is such a faith a gift that has been given to
you? The Bible gives us an immediate answer
to any spiritual uncertainty: anyone who receives
Christ is empowered to become a child of God
(John 1:12). The power that comes from God is
given to us in a very special way, according to the
apostle Paul:

> You were baptized into union with Christ, and
> now you are clothed, so to speak, with the life
> of Christ himself. So there is no difference
> between Jews and Gentiles, between slaves and
> free . . . between men and women; you are
> all one in union with Christ Jesus. If you
> belong to Christ, then you are the descendants
> of Abraham and will receive what God has
> promised. (Galatians 3:27-29, TEV)

Among God's promises, Paul points us to the power of the resurrection for the living of our life in Christ: "By our baptism, then, we were buried with him and shared his death, in order that, just as Christ was raised from death by the glorious power of the Father, so also we might live a new life" (Romans 6:4, TEV). The power to become faith-hardy children of God is God's gift to everyone called into the body of Christ. We have been baptized! We are God's own grace-gifted children!

Of course, in gifting us in this way, God intends our faith to make a definite difference in what we see and say and do. Accepting God's gift means not only treasuring it, but nourishing it. Just as good nutrition is needed to support the healthy functioning of our physical body, so spiritual nourishment is essential if we are to see with the eyes of faith and have the strength we need to take faith-hardy action.

THE CARE AND FEEDING OF FAITH

Christians throughout the history of the church have agreed on at least two crucial ingredients in an adequate spiritual diet: the word of God and the Lord's supper. Let's see how both of these help us toward a hardier, more confident faith.

Christ Jesus as the revealed word of God speaks to us and sustains us through the written and proclaimed word. In the Faith-Hardiness Inventory, those who say that Christ is present with them in a way that helps them see the challenges and choices in life are also those who are most likely to read the Bible as a spiritual discipline. How could it be otherwise? Who can read the Bible regularly without being met again and again by a God who not only cares, but cares enough to go all the way for his people? The Bible invites us to think of the ways in which the Lord is present in our life. It even helps us find the words to express our emotions at times when we feel alone and forsaken—but always in the context of hope. Even in the times of being alone, it is God who hears our cries.

Sometimes I get so busy that I fail to pick up the Bible except to find a text for something I am writing or a class I am teaching. If that happens for very many days, the scales begin to reappear on my eyes and I am not as conscious of the presence and care of Christ. God has given me the gift of faith and the gift of his written word. The one nourishes the other. My faith helps me rightly to understand what I read in the Bible, and what I read in the Bible strengthens me in my faith.

Our faith is also made hardier and more confident by hearing the proclaimed word. Proclamation is a group event—it takes at least two people or it can't happen. A sermon is a reminder that faith needs to be nourished not only in solitude, but also in relationship with other believers. To me, the most helpful sermons seem like they have emerged out of the very questions that I experience in the course of living my life. Sermons like that help me hear God's word to me in my situation. That my neighbor in the pew also feels as if the word were personally addressed to him or her simply strengthens my awareness that I am not alone in the struggles of faith—and my confidence that as Christ cares for me, so he cares for us all.

In addition to the written and proclaimed word, for Christians the celebration of the Lord's supper is another experience of special individual strengthening and corporate encouragement (Matthew 26:26-29; Mark 14:22-25; Luke 22:17-20; 1 Corinthians 11:23-26). The Lord's supper is intensely personal—"Take and eat," "This is my body, which is for you." For *you!*

During a stressful time in my life, or when I am scrambling to stay on top of my situation (or trying to let go), or when I am working through a loss that has left me feeling empty, or when I am in the midst of a conflict situation—receiving the Lord's supper gives me a most specific and concrete experience of Christ with me and for me. Growth in faith-hardiness is letting such experiences open our eyes to the way Christ's death and resurrection have transformed life and revealed its deeper meaning and purpose.

But that deeper meaning and purpose embraces more than myself. The Lord's supper is personal, but it is not at all a private affair. "Drink from it, all of you. This is my blood of the covenant, which is poured out for many for the forgiveness of sins" (Matthew 26:27-28). For *many!*

Christ is not only with me, as an individual Christian, he is with *us* as a family of faith. My (w)holistic model is meant to reflect the Bible's teaching about the interconnectedness and inter-relatedness of life. One of the ways I use that model is to remind myself that I cannot be healed or whole apart from the community of God's peo-ple, just as God's people cannot be whole apart from God. The peace of God *(shalom)* is a gift that calls us into an ever-deepening relationship with one another. Growth in faith-hardiness, then, is not taking place unless we are growing as responsible members of the church, the body of Christ.

SPIRITUAL CHALLENGES TO WORLD COMMUNITY

God's *shalom* is not the only reminder of the interrelatedness of life. The civil rights demon-strations and the Vietnam conflict of the 1960s, the nuclear disarmament debate of the 1970s and 1980s, and the return of the specter of geno-cide in the 1990s all show us, in profound and sometimes frightening ways, that what affects a part of humankind affects us all. Just as growth in faith-hardiness involves moving beyond the personal to the congregational, so it pulls us beyond the congregation into the community, the world, and even the cosmos.

How can the faith-hardy respond confidently to such changes as our modern world presents? First prayerfully, and then as Christ leads us. Regular prayer is as important for growth in faith-hardiness as is the disciplined reading of the Bible. In relationship problems, it is almost certain that there has been a breakdown in communication. Long before Kristin and Todd ran into trouble, they stopped having real conversations with each other. When Helen saw her communication with George getting weaker, she knew that other difficulties were not far behind. The fact is that friendships and marriages thrive on the listening and sharing that good communication involves. So does our relationship with God.

There is no one faith-hardy form of prayer, as long as our prayer serves the purpose of keeping the communication open and clear between our Lord and ourselves. Like George, sometimes I let my work be my prayer. One of the limitations of letting work be our prayer is that what we do keeps sending messages to Christ, but we may not be stopping long enough to listen to what he has to say to us. On the other hand, making a to-do about prayer but not translating what we hear from the Lord into action raises the question of whether or not we really listened very well at all.

I can't tell what is a faith-hardy prayer life for someone else, but for me it is when I live with a keen awareness of Christ being by my side. Sometimes in formal ways but often informally I tell him what I am thinking and feeling. Perhaps more importantly, since Christ already knows me better than I know myself, I listen for his guidance on how I might see things differently—and what I might do about what he helps me see.

When it comes to problems faced by the community, the nation, or the world, most of the time I am led by Christ to share those concerns with other Christians and with other persons, whether Christian or not, who care about people. Christian support groups, such as Elaine had, can be very valuable for thinking through problems and taking positive action. Support groups help not only with personal problems but also when we see something needing to be done that is more than any single person can do. Christ can also speak through the members of such groups so that our individual hearing of his word can be checked out with what others hear from him. There is always a chance that a little bit of our history or our life circumstance or our personality has interfered with our reception of the Lord's voice. Having a group of Christian friends can help us clear up such "static."

Can the faith-hardy really do anything about the larger, global issues that face humankind? Christian leaders and spokespersons from all denominations and in many countries continue to make very specific suggestions about what faithful people can do, if only we will. Unfortunately, many Christians are so overwhelmed by the enormity of the task that they give up on doing anything at all. Growth in faith-hardiness, however, means keeping yourself open to situations that need Christian ministry. Let the Christ at your side help you identify even one such situation as a personal or perhaps a congregational challenge. If every Christian had at least one larger concern and did his or her best to understand and respond to those needs, some wonderful things would happen. God never gives up on his people. Christ counts on the faith-hardy to embody his promise of presence where it is needed most. It is a broken and sinful world. But it is a world full of people God loves.

SUGGESTIONS FOR FAITH-HARDY GROWTH IN SPIRITUALITY

Keep in mind that a faith-hardy spirituality has Christ at the center. Whatever form our response to God's gift in Christ might take, our attention needs to remain centered on the Savior. Here are some ways that faith-hardy Christians keep growing.

Make sure your faith is being adequately fed. The forms of our worship or private devotions are not meant to get in the way of our experiencing the living Lord through them, but they can. If that happens, we become spiritually starved. Start first with your personal spiritual discipline, since that is the easiest to change. Think about what you do to strengthen yourself spiritually. Are you getting enough nourishment? If you are not, what is in the way? Are you setting aside enough time to communicate with Christ meaningfully? Are you feeding your faith regularly enough? The flowering of faith-hardiness is dependent on spiritual food at the root.

Give some thought to the possibility that spiritual growth for you might lie not only in your practicing the type of spirituality that comes to you naturally. George's attack led him to a new appreciation of Christian fellowship. Elaine might find it challenging to learn something about Christian meditation so she could grow in the faithful use of solitude. As we reach different stages in our life, an effort to balance our approach to spiritual discipline may prove to be very rewarding.

Be concerned not only about your own spiritual needs, but also those of others. Is your congregation sensitive to the variety of preferences and needs individual members have in making their response to Christ? If you are in a liturgical church with an order of service set by the denomination, there may be less flexibility. However, even in liturgical churches there are usually more options than you may realize. If there is a worship and music committee, you might consider joining it, or at least letting your thoughts be known.

Prepare yourself to hear God's word. Stay current with what is happening in the world and what is going on in your own life. What questions arise out of your experience? Bring those questions to your reading of the Bible. Take them with you as you attend worship and hear the sermon. Raise them in Sunday school. Be open to receiving an answer, but do not expect that answer according to some timetable you personally set. Sometimes I have not been ready to hear God's answer to certain questions until I had experienced a little more life. The faith-hardy live without specific answers to some questions because we trust that God's answer to the most critical question of life's meaning and purpose has already been given in Christ.

Take every opportunity to receive the Lord's supper. Since a faith-hardy perspective is grounded in our sense of Christ's presence with us and care for us, the confidence with which we face the changes and challenges of life can only increase as we are nourished through the Lord's supper.

Be prepared for Christ to let you know he is with you in unexpected ways. He is not bound by our traditions. Faith-hardiness grows as we look for Christ and are met by him in the most unlikely places and through the most surprising persons. Make it a habit to look for Christ as you encounter new people. But don't forget old friends and family members as well. Sometimes the Lord is even closer than we think. And he is never more than a prayer away. A new world is opened to us when God gives us the gift of seeing with the eyes of faith.

Remember that the new world that is opened to the faith-hardy is the whole world. Do you need to work on a more faithful balance between your interest and support for congregational ministry and the church's call to mission? It is very tempting, even for the faith-hardy, to take such good care of persons and needs close at hand that we forget that Jesus was always reaching out. How can you personally grow in letting the ministry you receive strengthen you for reaching out to others in the name of Christ?

We have now come near the end of our exploration of how to become a more faith-hardy, confident Christian. But being a caring and compassionate Christian as well, you may be wondering about what happened to the people you have met in this book.

Joe and Elaine thought and prayed a lot, Elaine talked it over with her friends and, along with Bobby, she and Joe had several meetings with their pastor. They finally came to the decision that Joe would take the transfer, but they would try to find a way for Bobby to remain in town for his final year of high school. One of the women in Elaine's church group offered a place for Bobby to stay, and the pastor volunteered to keep close contact. The year of separation was not without its difficulties, but it worked out for the best.

Kristin and Todd divorced when Todd did not return from out of state. Todd eventually contacted his daughters and did send Kristin the support money ordered by the court, though not regularly. Kristin did not remarry for some years. She was encouraged by the helpful talks with her pastor to enter professional counseling. There she dealt with her feelings about her marital breakup and regained some of her lost self-esteem. An associates degree that she was able to get by taking classes part-time in a community college landed her a position at the general hospital.

After Helen gained the courage to tell George how desperately she missed the relationship they had had before George's heart attack and how angry she was that he had pulled back so far, she was relieved to find that George accepted her feelings quite well. He acknowledged that he missed their closeness, too, but that being close made him feel vulnerable. Their physician was able to help George deal with his anxiety about physical intimacy, but his problem with vulnerability took more time. As it does with many Christians, such a close brush with death raised all kinds of issues that had to be sorted out. You will recall that during one of the pastor's calls George was in the process of doing some of that sorting. A lot more needed to be done. The pastor's special support ministry to both George and Helen continued for more than a year. When George and Helen finally accepted the change in their lives as a challenge their Lord would help them meet day by day, they recaptured their feeling of being together—in love and in Christ.

Through the stories of these persons, I have shared with you a perspective on the Christian faith. What I have called faith-hardiness is simply living our life in the confidence of the faith that Christ is right beside us every step of the way. It is a powerful, Christ-centered way of looking at life, the power of hopeful, positive, transformative "seeing," a power that is not our own but a gift from God. Seeing with the eyes of faith transforms the ordinary into the extraordinary as we see every person as gifted by God in special ways and as we courageously and confidently approach every challenge trusting that Christ is present and caring. It is that simple.

Except, as we have seen in the lives of Elaine, Joe, Bobby, Kristin, Todd, George, and Helen, sometimes the living out of such a faith is not so simple. Our histories, our personalities, and our life situations can get in the way of our really feeling that Christ is present with us and for us. But our backgrounds, our personal preferences, and our circumstances do not have to be barriers. They can be the very means through which our Lord chooses to speak if only we will listen.

I hope this book has provided you with some ideas of how to let what is going on in your life help you to hear Christ's voice. I also hope that you have been encouraged to face the "ventures of which we cannot see the ending," and all other challenges in your life with faith-hardy confidence, knowing that God's hand is leading us and God's love is supporting us through the presence and care of Christ our Lord.

FAITH-HARDINESS INVENTORY

On most of the following questions, circle a number from 1 to 5, depending on which number best reflects how you think, feel, or act. For example, on the first question you are asked about your physical health. A person in excellent physical health would circle the number 1. A person in very poor physical health would circle the number 5. People who have neither excellent nor very poor health will, of course, circle a number in between. For instance, "good" health might be a 2.

Now, giving an honest estimate of yourself, respond to the following:

1. At what level would you assess your physical health at the present time?

    excellent   1 2 3 4 5   very poor

2. However you define it, at what level would you assess your sense of *psychological* well-being at the present time?

    very high   1 2 3 4 5   very low

3. However you define it, at what level would you assess your sense of *spiritual* well-being at the present time?

   very high   1 2 3 4 5   very low

4. With *all* factors considered (personal and family relationships, work, health, finances, etc.), if you were to take a stress test covering the past year, where do you think you would score?

very calm and relaxed	1 2 3 4 5	very highly stressed

5. Regardless of the number of stressful events they experience, people are different in how stressed they subjectively *feel*. Generally speaking, are you

very calm and relaxed	1 2 3 4 5	very highly stressed

6. When it comes to saying no, are you

able to say no in a way that does not alienate	1 2 3 4 5	unable to say no or unable to say no unless angry

Faith-Hardiness Inventory is copyright © 1984 Gary L. Harbaugh, Ph.D.

7. When you are faced with a change in life circumstances, are you

more open to the new possibilities	1 2 3 4 5	more aware of what is being left behind

8. When you are in a situation of interpersonal conflict (home, work, congregation), are you more likely to

view conflict as a possible way to make things better	1 2 3 4 5	view conflict as a threat and potentially destructive

9. In a loss situation, or a time of major change, such as serious illness, accident, job loss, retirement, separation, divorce, etc., are you

confident that the future will be better	1 2 3 4 5	more conscious of what has been lost or changed

10. When things are changing around you, do you usually

feel able to keep things under control	1 2 3 4 5	feel unable to maintain control

11. If you assess your needs to be in control, how important is it for you to be "on top of the situation"?

I can let go easily	1 2 3 4 5	I need to be in control

12. Personally, are you more inclined to be

generally open and trusting of others	1 2 3 4 5	more cautious and not very self-disclosing

13. When times are tough, are you usually able to discern the "meaning" or purpose of a difficult situation?

usually very insightful and I keep my perspective	1 2 3 4 5	usually I get bogged down in the details of the problem

14. Is your personal, devotional life a resource to you as you deal with personal and professional frustrations, conflicts, and pressures?

yes, a major source of comfort and direction	1 2 3 4 5	no, my devotional life is not a resource at present

15. To be a person involves body, mind, feelings, relationships, and ultimate values. Please *rank* the following from 1 to 5, with the most *important* for you being number 1:

    ___ physical
    ___ mental
    ___ emotional
    ___ social
    ___ spiritual

16. "Self-care" involves a balanced approach to life with adequate rest, relaxation, exercise, nutrition, personal growth activities, etc. Taking into account both information *and* practice, at what level would you rate your self-care at the present time?

    informed   uninformed
    and skilled   1 2 3 4 5   and unskilled

17. Please check any of the following forms of self-care that you *regularly* practice:

    ___ physical exercise, jogging, fast walking, etc.
    ___ balanced nutrition
    ___ relaxation techniques, biofeedback, etc.
    ___ time management (prioritize, limit hours, time off)
    ___ self-help reading
    ___ personal support group(s)
    ___ disciplined personal Bible reading
    ___ personal prayer and other private devotions

___ worship and other corporate religious
    practices

___ other _____

18. How do you *usually* perceive change?

a challenge and an opportunity	1 2 3 4 5	an obstacle or a danger

19. When you are in a stressful situation, how do you *usually* perceive yourself?

a person with real choices and options	1 2 3 4 5	a person with very limited choices and options

20. In a difficult situation lasting more than a few days, how conscious are you of Christ's presence and care?

very real presence and care	1 2 3 4 5	not aware, or aware only in later reflection

SCORING THE
FAITH-HARDINESS INVENTORY

Your responses to the Faith-Hardiness Inventory results in three "scores." The first is a "Well-Being" score. To find your Well-Being score, add together your answers to questions 1, 2, and 3. For example, if on the first question (physical health) you answered with a 3, on the second question (psychological well-being) a 2, and on the third question (spiritual well-being) a 1, your Well-Being score would be a 3 + 2 + 1 = 6. The average Well-Being score for all who have taken the Faith-Hardiness Inventory is about 6. The more faith-hardy average a score of about 4.

WELL-BEING

Add your responses to questions 1, 2, and 3. Now, find your Well-Being score and write it in here:

Questions $\overline{1}$ + $\overline{2}$ + $\overline{3}$ = $\overline{\text{Well-Being}}$

WHOLENESS

The second score you can determine from the Faith-Hardiness Inventory is a "Wholeness" score. To find this, add your answers to numbers 6–14, skip 15, then add 16. The average Wholeness score is about 24 for males and 27 for females. Both faith-hardy men and women average about 20.

Questions $\overline{6}$ + $\overline{7}$ + $\overline{8}$ + $\overline{9}$ + $\overline{10}$ + $\overline{11}$ +

$\overline{12}$ + $\overline{13}$ + $\overline{14}$ + $\overline{16}$ = $\overline{\text{Wholeness}}$

FAITH-HARDINESS

The third score is the sum of your answers to the final three questions (numbers 18–20). This is your Faith-Hardiness score. The average Faith-Hardiness score is about 7. The more faith-hardy usually score 5 or less.

$$\overline{\text{Questions }} \quad \overline{18} + \overline{19} + \overline{20} = \overline{\text{Faith-Hardiness}}$$

Most of the other questions in the Faith-Hardiness Inventory are about stress, your reaction to stress, and how you try to manage it. Check to see if there is any difference in your answers to how you think you would score on a stress test and how stressed you actually *feel* (questions 4 and 5).

After checking your stress scores, then see what you actually *do* about that stress. Is your self-care rating (question 16) consistent with the kind and number of things you regularly do to take care of yourself (question 17)?

The one remaining question asks you to rank the physical, mental, emotional, and social dimensions according to how important each is to you. This is a way to remind us that faith-hardiness has to do with ourselves as *whole* persons. If you had some question about how to rank the spiritual, it may be because the spiritual does not really belong on a list as if the spiritual were only a *part* of us. In chapters 1, 2, and 6 we shall see how the spiritual is better understood as the integrating *center* of our lives as *whole persons* in Christ.

REFERENCES AND RECOMMENDED READING

Psychological hardiness is an important concept for Christians to understand. For more on hardiness see the work of Salvatore R. Maddi and Suzanne C. Kobasa, *The Hardy Executive* (Homewood, Ill.: Dow Jones-Irwin, 1984). Other references and recommended readings include:

Arnold, William V. *The Power of Your Perceptions.* Philadelphia: Westminster, 1984. From the series Potentials: Guides for Productive Living, Wayne E. Oates, ed.

Augsburger, David W. *Anger and Assertiveness in Pastoral Care.* Philadelphia: Fortress, 1979.

Becker, Arthur H. *The Compassionate Visitor.* Augsburg, 1985.

Benson, Herbert. *Beyond the Relaxation Response.* New York: Times Books, 1984.

———. *The Relaxation Response.* New York: Wings Books, 1992.

Carmody, John. *Holistic Spirituality*. New York: Paulist, 1984.

Clinebell, Howard. *Growth Counseling* and selected chapters in *Basic Types of Pastoral Care and Counseling*. Nashville: Abingdon, 1979 (out of print) and 1984.

Davidson, Glen W. *Understanding Mourning*. Minneapolis: Augsburg, 1984.

Emmons, Michael, and Richardson, David. *The Assertive Christian*. Minneapolis: Winston, 1981.

Grant, W. Harold, Thompson, Magdala, and Clarke, Thomas E. *From Image to Likeness: A Jungian Path in the Gospel Journey*. Ramsey, N.J.: Paulist, 1983.

Harbaugh, Gary L. "Anger Gives Signals." Augsburg Leaflet Ministry (1985).

———. "Change and the 'Hardy' Pastor." *LCA Partners* 6 (December 1984–January 1985).

———. *God's Gifted People,* Expanded Edition. Minneapolis: Augsburg, 1990.

———. *Pastor as Person*. Minneapolis: Augsburg, 1984. This book can be useful for laypersons, both for self-understanding and for appreciating the personal concerns of the clergy and their families.

———. "The Person in Ministry." *Trinity Seminary Review* (Spring 1983); and "A Model for Caring." *Thanatos* (1983). (These articles cite the (w)holistic model, original copyright 1968, 1976, 1983.)

———. "Praying Stress Away." *The Lutheran* (July 1984). An example of how to integrate stress reduction and spirituality. See also chapter 6 of *Pastor as Person.*

Harbaugh, Gary L., Brenneis, Rebecca Lee, and Hutton, Rodney R. *Covenants and Care.* Minneapolis: Fortress Press, 1998.

Haugk, Kenneth C. *Christian Caregiving—A Way of Life.* Minneapolis: Augsburg, 1984.

Holmes, T. H. and Rahe, R. H. "The Social Readjustment Rating Scale." *Journal of Psychosomatic Research* 11 (April 1967): 213–18.

Hulme, William E. *Managing Stress in Ministry.* San Francisco: Harper & Row, 1985.

Hulme, William E., Brekke, Milo, and Behrens, William C., eds. *Pastors in Ministry.* Minneapolis: Augsburg, 1985.

Keller, John. *Let Go, Let God.* Minneapolis: Augsburg, 1985.

Lange, Arthur J., and Jakubowski, Patricia. *Responsible Assertive Behavior: Cognitive-Behavioral Procedures for Trainers.* Champaign, Ill.: Research Press, 1976.

Lester, Andrew D. *Coping with Your Anger: A Christian Guide.* Philadelphia: Westminster, 1983.

Marty, Martin E. *A Cry of Absence.* San Francisco: Harper & Row, 1983.

Miller, Mark A., and Rahe, Richard H. "Life Changes Scaling for the 1990s." *Journal of Psychosomatic Research.* 43 (1997): 279–92. The

Social Readjustment Rating Scale was developed by Drs. Thomas Holmes and Richard Rahe and first published in 1965. The version used in this book represents its most recent form to date, updated and rescaled, as published in 1997 (see citation above). Used by permission.

Miller, William R. *Living As If: How Positive Faith Can Change Your Life*. Philadelphia: Westminster, 1985.

Myers, Isabel Briggs, and Myers, Peter B. *Gifts Differing*. Palo Alto, Calif.: Consulting Psychologists Press, 1980. The best single book to read for a better understanding of the Myers-Briggs Type Indicator.®

Oswald, Roy M. *Clergy Burnout*. Alban Institute: Ministers Life Resource, 1982.

———. *Clergy Self-Care: Finding a Balance for Effective Ministry*. Bethesda, Md.: Alban Institute, 1991.

Page, Earle C. "Finding Your Spiritual Path." Gainesville, Fla.: Center for Applications of Psychological Type, 1982.

Pines, Maya. "Psychological Hardiness: The Role of Challenge in Health." *Psychology Today* 14 (December 1980).

Randall, Robert L. *Putting the Pieces Together: The Guidance of a Pastoral Psychologist*. New York: Pilgrim Press, 1986.

Rassieur, Charles L. *Stress Management for Ministers*. Philadelphia: Westminster, 1982.

Sehnert, Keith. *Stress/Unstress* and *Selfcare/Well-care*. Minneapolis: Augsburg, 1981 and 1985.

Steinke, Peter. *Healthy Congregations: A Systems Approach*. Bethesda, Md.: Alban Institute, 1996.

Tagliaferre, Lewis, and Harbaugh, Gary. *Recovery from Loss*. Deerfield Beach, Fla.: Health Communications, 1990.

Tournier, Paul. Any of the writings of this Swiss physician will provide readers powerful, faithful insights, but especially helpful to me in my life have been: *The Meaning of Persons*. New York: Harper & Row, 1982. *The Whole Person in a Broken World*. Harper & Row, 1981. A good overview of Tournier's thought can be found in *Reflections: A Personal Guide for Life's Most Crucial Questions*. Philadelphia: Westminster, 1982.

Tubesing, Donald A., and Tubesing, Nancy Loving. *The Caring Question*. Minneapolis: Augsburg, 1984.

Westberg, Granger E. *Good Grief*. Philadelphia: Fortress, 1962. Dr. Westberg has also authored influential guidelines on how to develop (w)holistic health in congregations.

Wold, Erling, and Wold, Margaret. See their series of inspirational books, including *What Do I Have to Do . . . Break My Neck?* and *Thanks for the Mountain*. Augsburg, 1974 and 1975. (Out of print.)